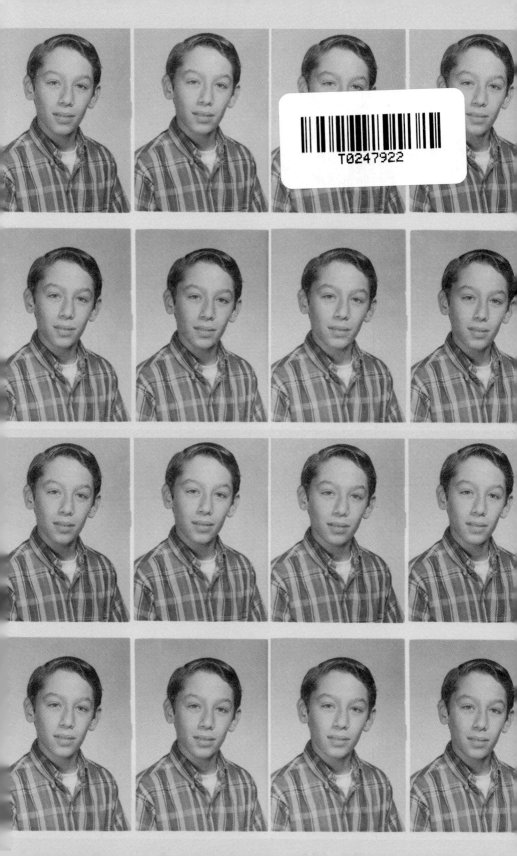

BROTHERS

ALEX VAN HALEN

HARPER

An Imprint of HarperCollins*Publishers*

HarperCollins books may be purchased for educational, business, or sales promotional use. For information, please email the Special Markets Department at SPsales@harpercollins.com.

FIRST EDITION

All images courtesy of the author except where otherwise noted.

Designed by Bonni Leon-Berman

Library of Congress Cataloging-in-Publication Data has been applied for.

ISBN 978-0-06-326570-7

24 25 26 27 28 LBC 5 4 3 2 1

TO STINE VAN HALEN, THE LOVE OF MY LIFE

BROTHERS

OVERTURE

Without my brother, I would not be. We fight, argue—we even argue about agreeing on things—but there is a bond and unconditional love that very few people ever experience in their lifetime. We're not a rock band. We're a rock 'n' roll band. Alex is the rock. I'm the roll.

—EDWARD VAN HALEN (1955–2020)

Music was our heart and soul. That's what we did. That's what we loved. That's what we enjoyed and what we were good at. It was also the thing that made us as close as two brothers can be. We were connected in every way—genetically, artistically, financially, emotionally, and though neither of us stuck with Catholicism, I'm going to go ahead and say spiritually. It's very difficult to unwind that. It's been almost four years since you passed, Ed, but sometimes it feels like it just happened this morning.

One of my earliest memories—I couldn't have been more than two—is of our mother telling me to be quiet so I wouldn't wake you, my new baby brother. You weren't just younger. You were more introverted, more impressionable, and more sensitive than I was, always. "Wear a suit!" Mom would shout, no matter how successful we got. I didn't care; it would just roll off me. I guess I'm tough?

"You make a living beating things with a stick, what do you ex-pect?" That's what you said, and I guess you were right.

You couldn't filter out criticism—or adulation, for that matter; everything just got right to you. People always talk about that smile of yours, the smile of a little kid . . . open. It wasn't just the way you looked. That was you.

That sensitivity is part of what made you a brilliant musician. "The world's greatest guitarist" is what everyone says, but it's kind of a dicey title—you never liked it. I can tell you this much: saying you're the "greatest" implies there were many more like you. But there was only one Edward Van Halen.

You could play just a single note and it sounded different, dis-tinct. Miles Davis said it's not the notes, it's the intent . . . it's that intangible essence that makes the difference between one sound and another. From the first time you picked up a guitar—my guitar, actually—the resonance and intonation were unique. Long before people were going crazy for your finger tapping, the talent was already there, even when you just played a chord. You always said you didn't know where it came from.

People tell me, "You'll always have the music." And the best tribute anyone can give you is to listen to our songs. (I'm listening to "Loss of Control" as I write this.) It's the stuff in between the licks that gets me—it's so particular, such a distinctive way of playing you had . . . and then within seconds you've already changed the lick! You've let it evolve, ever so slightly, in the most interesting way. And you weren't even aware of it half the time. Music just came through you.

But I watched you take your last breath. In that moment, all the stuff that you did or made in this world . . . you can't take it with you.

Since you've been gone, I catch myself talking to you (yelling at you) in my head, or sometimes out loud. I still have trouble believing you're gone—and probably for me, you never will be. Outliving my little brother? This just wasn't the plan. As the older brother, I was supposed to die first. Same as always, Ed: butting in line!

I've watched—sometimes with anger, sometimes with grief, and other times with pride—as the world has mourned your passing and other people have claimed to tell your story. But I was with you from day one. We shared the experience of coming to this country and figuring out how to fit in. We shared a record player, an eight-hundred-square-foot house, a mom and dad, and a work ethic. Later, we shared the back of a tour bus, the experience of becoming successful, of becoming fathers and uncles, of alcoholism, and of spending more hours in the studio than I've spent doing anything else in this life. We shared a depth of understanding that most people can only hope to achieve.

We shared a last name. And we shared a band.

And here's what I have to say.

ONE

In the beginning, God created Van Halen with a little help from Ed and Al. And the people saw that it was good! A celebration of life and everything it means to be human. Now that I've got your attention . . .

However you start our story, it starts with music. Even if you start before we were born. Our father, Jan Van Halen, was a Dutch musician who'd played all over Europe in orchestras and jazz groups. When World War II broke out, he joined the Dutch air force and they had him play in the marching band. He was proud of that, as he should have been. He never talked about what came next: The Germans invaded Holland in 1940 and conscripted the entire Dutch army. If you refused, they shot you dead on the spot. So the next thing he knows, my father is being forced to play German oompah music and propaganda songs, more or less with a gun to his head.

When the war was over, Dad went to Indonesia for a six-week gig at a radio station on the island of Java. That's where he met our mother, Ottie. He ended up staying six years.

Mom—whose proper name was Eugenia—was an Indonesian girl who grew up with a dozen siblings and almost as many maids in a big house. They were wealthy because my grandfather had invested in the railroad, but it was still seen as a move up the ladder to marry a white guy. Usually.

You have to understand, our dad wasn't a regular white guy. First, he was a musician, so already that's not so good. Plus, he and his buddies drank a lot, so that's strike two. He drove a Norton motor-cycle, and the first time he put our mother on the back of it, she was so little and light that she flew right off. Dad was fun and he was handsome, and women loved him. Mom married him on August 11, 1950.

Now, this was just a year after Indonesia gave its colonizer, Holland, the finger and said, "Hey! We're grown-ass men and women, and we don't want you around here anymore telling us what to do!" Consequently, white Dutch guys like my dad weren't partic-ularly popular or welcome, and he was having a hard time getting any work. So, not long after they married, Mom left her homeland to go and live in Dad's.

IF YOU START OUR STORY with our childhood in Holland, you're still starting with music.

I remember the *boom boom boom* of the pile drivers—that was like the soundtrack of my early childhood. They're always trying to claim back land from the water in the Netherlands, so that percussive sound was ever-present. I can still hear it in my head. Maybe that's why I became a drummer.

When I came along on May 8, 1953, and Ed joined the party twenty months later, my mother was determined to make us re-spectable in all the ways her husband wasn't. A big piece of her plan was classical music: that's why my brother's name was Edward

Lodewijk Van Halen. (That's Dutch for Ludwig, as in Beethoven— whose real last name was *van* Beethoven, just by the way.) We had a Rippen upright piano, and Mom made us take lessons and—this became a sore spot—we weren't allowed to leave the house unless we'd practiced.

Ed and I were both good at it, and my mother was very proud of our ability, and very intense in her ambitions for us. She *really* wanted us to be well educated and white-collar someday: she was hoping for concert pianists playing Carnegie Hall, not Van Halen with the Monsters of Rock.

"My dad, who was a musician, didn't push us at all. My mom was the one pushing us," Ed once told a journalist. "You know the father in the movie *Shine*? That's what my mom was like." *Shine* is a biopic about the Australian pianist David Helfgott, whose father teaches him to play and then rides his ass mercilessly over the slightest error or sign of disobedience. The dad is the villain of the film, totally abusive. Helfgott eventually went nuts. It's a pretty harsh comparison.

The Rippen piano is parked in my hallway now. I see it every time I leave the kitchen and I think of my mother—tiny but tough. There was a little room under the stairs in our flat in Holland and there was always the threat that if you were bad, she'd send you there, put you in solitary. It was dark in there and it smelled bad. Completely freaked me out.

Dad played clarinet and saxophone, but he could play any woodwind instrument, and he was always touring around Northern Europe to gigs. His band, the Ton Wijkamp Quintet, headlined the annual Loosdrecht Jazz Festival—it's like the Dutch version of our Jazz Fest in New Orleans; it's still going on.

When Ed and I were little there was no television, so you lived in your imagination—that and roughhousing kept us busy. We lived in Nijmegen, a town near the German border that the United States had bombed the hell out of while the Nazis occupied Holland. Dad used to play us these recordings he'd made with the Dutch air force band during the first year of the war, and Ed and I would march around the table listening to them, for literally hours on end. It taught us early the power of music, how it can entrain you.

WE LIVED IN A FLAT in a block of six apartment buildings and one of my mom's sisters lived next door. That was our world: the flats, the church, the school. The rest didn't exist. It was always cold in the flat; for a while the only heat came from a little hot water boiler in the kitchen. Once, when I was a baby, my mother put me in my bassinet right next to it to keep me warm, and then went to do something. When she came back in I'd turned blue. The pilot light had blown out and, basically, I'd been gassed. I probably lost half my brain cells that morning . . . been looking for them ever since.

Ed and I were baptized and raised Catholic to satisfy our mother, and back then, you didn't go over to the Protestant side of town. Our dad didn't care for organized religion. He didn't like to talk about the war much, but one thing he told us many times was that when he was stationed in London and the bombs started falling, people didn't pray: they went to the basement to party like there was no tomorrow. That's always stuck with me. And it tells you a lot about his view of what's holy, what matters. "My father, two things he always says are: 'You only live once,'" said my brother, "and 'There's nothing better than a good life.'"

He knew how to have fun, how to lead the charge. Now that Mom's gone I can admit my dad was . . . let's call it an "incurable romantic." He had a way with women. I tried not to see this growing up, but it's something that Ed and I both knew.

My parents were old-world and old-school. They didn't baby us. Dad had a footlocker in which he kept his air force uniform and a twenty-five-clip submachine gun. We played with both. It's one of my earliest memories, fiddling with that gun, so I would have been only five or six.

In Holland, the men we knew did two things: work and drink. Other musicians would come by our flat, or my father's two brothers and their wives, and things would get rowdy from time to time. My dad was a very gentle, tender, soft-spoken guy, until he drank. Then he was the life of the party. My mom, on the other hand, never touched alcohol. Sometimes, when he came home from a long day—or night—of work, wanted to blow off steam, and had a few too many, she would start in on him: why don't you do this or that and wear a suit and be an upstanding member of society? That's all she wanted.

Three of my mother's sisters had moved to Holland, and I think there was always a little competition over who married best. My aunt Deedee in the flat next door thought she was the big cheese because her husband was an executive at Coca-Cola, and he was always bringing home bottles of the stuff. Pretty soon my cousins had rotten Coca-Cola teeth. (Not like we had anything to brag about in that department: Ed and I didn't see a dentist until we were sixteen; our parents couldn't afford it. So how are my teeth? Perfect. They've all been replaced!)

My cousins didn't like us because Ed and I were lucky enough to be born with a talent, and they weren't. My mom had us play at every possible opportunity—which made us the center of attention at family gatherings, and the objects of envy. I didn't want to hang out with them anyway: if I was going to hang around with girls, I didn't want them to be blood relations. We had some kind of skirmish with them at some point. Plus my dad came home drunk one night and their father knocked my old man down the steps. We didn't see them anymore after that.

My mom had yet another sister, living just outside of Los Angeles, who kept writing us letters about how beautiful it was— just like Java, she said. The weather was incredible; oranges were only a penny. It sounded good to my mom, and to tell you the truth it sounded pretty good to me: I hated the cold. Still do.

I don't know how much this played into it, but my mom felt like people looked down on us in Holland because she was Indonesian. Don't forget: she was dying to be respectable. Well, that's never happening if everybody around you thinks you don't deserve any respect because you're a foreigner. She thought we'd have a better life in California, a shot at the American Dream. It was a "nation of immigrants," so how could anybody be racist, right? Theoretically, anyway, everybody was equal.

And my dad? He was adaptable. He was up for anything. The guy had been through the Second World War and seen the camps. Nothing fazed him.

IF YOU START OUR STORY in 1962 with the two-week boat ride from Holland to America, you can probably guess what I remember about it: music.

I was eight and Ed was six, and our father got us a gig. We were the freak show piano-playing little kids who got to sit at the captain's table after we performed—my dad had negotiated it as a form of payment. My attitude was, *I'm taking over here.* (I was overly confident as a kid . . . and maybe as a young man.) We'd been in the bowels of the boat, in third class, and two days later we were up in first, sitting with the captain, making it our regular place to hang out. It was just our nature, the way we did things: always looking for an angle.

There was a little girl on that boat, dark haired, cute, and man, I was smitten. It's my first memory of being overtaken by that feeling—you don't know why, or where it comes from, but suddenly there it is. I thought I had two weeks to convince her that I was her knight. Then she got off the boat in London. I was devastated. That was the biggest disappointment of that trip.

The other thing I remember is the smell on that boat—not fishy, not like a hotel or a house, a distinctive *boat smell.* That's the only way I can describe it, and it'll be with me my whole life. Two weeks is a long time for kids out in the middle of the ocean.

When we got to New York, they figured out that our piano had somehow been lost from the cargo hold. My dad said, "Let's just stay here, we can live in New York." But my mom was determined: we have a sponsor and a place to stay in Pasadena, and besides, oranges are a cent apiece. She was from the tropics—those oranges loomed large.

So we took a train across the country. It was called the Dreamliner, and the car in the middle had a big skylight— "the Great Dome," where you could watch the trees and the buildings going by. I remember Ed telling me, "You missed the Indians, man!" when I woke up from a rest. Apparently, when we pulled into Phoenix or some town out west, they had guys dressed up in feathers get on top of the train. (It was a different time.) I couldn't believe Ed hadn't woken me up for it. I was probably pissed at him all the way through Nevada.

It was a four-day trip and the main topic of discussion for a lot of it was whether we should get off in Chicago. My dad was for it, but my mother held firm: "No, no, no, we're going to LA because that's where my family is." When we finally got there—still in our big-ass winter coats from Holland—it was blazing hot. And my uncle came to pick us up in a baby-blue '56 Ford convertible. Ed and I were looking at that car thinking, *We've arrived!* You don't have cars like that in Holland. You don't have weather like that in Holland. Northern Europe is relentlessly, aggressively gray. In Southern California, everything was bright as hell. It was spectacular, overwhelming, like we'd come to a totally different universe—like Dorothy waking up in Oz instead of Kansas, taking in the Technicolor. I thought, *This is the shit. I'm never leaving.* And I never have.

Ed and I were mesmerized. At first, we stayed in a triplex with my uncle, a good piano player and a really sweet guy, who was married to my mother's loosest sister—every family has one of those. There was only one bathroom for the three apartments and in my infinite wisdom I hung a sign on it that said "Out of Order," thinking then everyone would have to go find another one and I'd always have it to myself.

American culture was brain-bending and completely absorbing. We couldn't believe the cartoons! In Holland you only got TV for like twenty minutes, once a week, back then. It seemed like Felix the Cat was on the black-and-white TV all the time in California. We couldn't get enough of it . . . which was a good thing because while everyone else was at work—or, in my parents' case, looking for it—Ed and I were alone with the cartoons. They'd leave at seven in the morning and tell us, "Just keep the TV on this channel and we'll see you at four." Okay. We can do that.

For a while, my mom got a job working as a domestic, and my dad was doing shifts as a janitor. Not exactly the California Dream. Dad started working at a machine shop, too, a job a cousin of ours got for him. Unfortunately, he also got thrown in jail after we'd been in California for only two weeks.

He was working the swing shift—from four in the afternoon until about two in the morning—and he got a ride home with some co-workers. They were pulled over for a broken taillight. My father used to roll his own cigarettes, and he was in the middle of doing that when the officer put his head in the window. The cop saw the rolling papers and the loose tobacco on my father's lap and asked if it was marijuana. My dad didn't speak any English so he just nodded his head. And of course they took him in.

We had no idea where he was at first, and even once we knew he was in jail, we didn't understand that someone was supposed to go and bail him out. That's not how it works in Holland—where we were familiar with the system. My dad had been thrown in the can there from time to time, for drunk and disorderly conduct, stuff like that.

Nobody in the family explained bail to us in California. (Don't forget: my mom had married a white guy.) After fifteen days, we finally figured it out and went and got my dad. If my mom was irritated with her sister for being less than forthcoming, she hid it. The fact was that it was my aunt's support that got us out here to California, and she had two sons not that far in age from me and Ed. But we never really played much, and after the first month or two, we went our own way.

IF YOU START OUR STORY when Ed and I were two little Dutch kids who didn't speak a word of English and had to find a way to fit into elementary school in Pasadena, our new home, you know we did that with music.

One of the first things I remember about our new school, McKinley Elementary, is that all the Black kids—maybe thirty—were in one class. I couldn't figure out why that was. I didn't ask, though. At that age, you take for granted that whatever you see is just the way it is. Plus, we had just come to a new country; I didn't know what the rules were here. Well, the rules in the early sixties in Pasadena were still de facto segregation.

That entry into an alien, unfamiliar life together sealed the bond between me and Ed. "We were two outcasts that didn't speak the language and didn't know what was going on," Ed has said. "So we became best friends and learned to stick together." The intimacy was permanent. But we weren't outcasts for long.

Fortunately for us, the schools in Europe were much more advanced than the schools in the United States, so we started with an academic advantage. (And I was exaggerating—we did know *one* word in English: "accident." It was the first word in the alphabetized "how to learn English" book my mom had brought on the boat.) The other thing we had going for us was that Ed and I were both athletic. Baseball, basketball—as you might imagine, Ed had amazing hand-eye coordination; he was second to none in that regard. But he was fast, too, did really well in track and field. His best event was the fifty-yard dash, sprinting. I was the miler, the long-distance guy. (Representative of our different personalities: I'm the rock, he's the roll. Ed could never sit still. He was always wolfing down breakfast, for instance. *What's the hurry? We've got a long day ahead of us. Let's not use up all our energy before we leave the house!*) Eventually we became "squad leaders," which basically meant you got to wear a red bandana around your waist and tell people what to do. But that was later. When we first got to America, socially, music smoothed it all over for us.

After my parents were able to get us our own place, Ed and I made friends with a pair of brothers who lived up the block— Brian and Kevin. Everywhere we went, we made friends with guys who were brothers: Greg and David; Ross and Bill; Brian and Kevin. They came in pairs. Ed would befriend the younger one, and I would befriend the older one. Brian and Kevin knew nothing about music, but they had a plastic Emenee guitar and that was a big attraction for us. We'd been playing drums on empty Baskin-Robbins ice cream containers and using a shoebox with a paper towel roll taped to its ass for a guitar. A plastic toy was a step up. What was even better was that Brian and Kevin had an older brother with an actual drum set, and sometimes we'd get our hands on it.

That's what I remember about our early days in Pasadena. Ed saw it differently. "It was beyond frightening," he once told a journalist. "We had to go to school and Al and I didn't know anything about anything." (Like I said, Ed was more sensitive than I am.) "Our struggle to make it in America made us stronger, because you had to be."

My dad started playing with a bunch of other Dutch guys he met in the area. (It's a funny thing about humans: we move halfway around the world just to surround ourselves with other people from where we started out.) They were all excellent musicians and true professionals individually, but together, as a band, they were *smoking*. Even so, they had a hard time finding work, and they often ended up just playing at the local Dutch club. I'm not saying it was an embarrassment, but it was way below their level.

Our mother may have forced us to learn piano, but our father taught us about musicianship by example. I remember sitting in the room with him watching him make his own reeds. To get the proper tone and feel and fit for his mouthpiece, he would shave them with a plane and then smooth them with sandpaper. Then he would just sit there in a room playing the same note for an hour to get it exactly right. Woodwind instruments are affected by humidity, temperature, all kinds of things. Most clarinet players have a really glassy sound, but our father had a woody sound—a richer, earthier tone—and that didn't happen by accident. (Later, this would influence what Ed and I called the "brown sound" that we were going for.) My father would sit there, totally absorbed in what he was doing. His whole world became the reed in his mouth.

What I learned from that is *focus on what you're doing right now*, even if it doesn't look important, because it all affects your sound. And as a musician, your sound is your identity. It was sort of indirectly hammered into us from the very beginning: when you play, it needs to sound like *you*, because that's your voice.

For three years in a row, Ed and I won first place in our respective age categories at the Long Beach City College classical piano contest, beating out thousands of other little contestants. "There's always a difference between a person who has the feel and those who don't. The difference is the amount of emotion expressed in your playing," Ed said. "I listened to Debussy by two different pianists and it was like day and night." Obviously, all this winning, this acclaim, thrilled my mom. Our teacher was a brilliant man who'd studied at the Imperial Conservatory in Saint Petersburg, Russia, and used to whack our hands with his ruler if we made a mistake. "The funny thing is, I never learned how to read music—I fooled the teacher," Ed said once. "I was just blessed with good ears; I'd watch his fingers and emulate what he did. He didn't find out till much later that I couldn't read, one time when he was playing a new piece of music and he asked me to turn the page for him. This was after like *five years* of lessons with the guy that he finally found out, which he wasn't too happy about."

The real issue was that classical piano never felt like Ed's voice, and it didn't feel like mine, either. "We had to learn to play piano because that was the 'respectable' instrument," as Ed put it. "It was my mom's dream." But it wasn't ours. The last thing we wanted to sound was respectable. "When we came to the US, I heard Jimi Hendrix and Cream, and I said, 'Forget the piano. I don't want to sit down. I want to stand up and be crazy!'"

Naturally, Van Halen's two biggest hits ended up being key-board tunes: "Jump" and "Right Now." You try everything and then in the end you listen to your mother! She gave us guilt about it for years, but Ed and I both drifted away from the Rippen upright. This was some pretty conspicuous neglect, because the Rippen—which was *destroyed* when it finally arrived in Pasadena, had to be completely put back together—was the centerpiece of our eight-hundred-square-foot household.

It was tight at our place. I can picture every inch of it: In the living room, you had the piano and the TV, and years later my drum kit and Ed's amps. Eventually, there was also this massive organ with a rhythm box in it that my mom would play—on holidays, she'd pound out the oldies with my dad accompanying her on sax. Next was the kitchen, and then Ed's "bedroom," which was really just a foyer to the back door. He had absolutely no privacy—if you wanted to enter or leave our house, you did it through Ed's room. The next door over was our folks' bedroom, and then if you walked a little farther, you got to my space: an add-on to the house made of plywood so flimsy it was more like cardboard; you could put your foot through it without even trying. It was on a concrete slab and it had no heat, nothing. Both Ed's room and my room had distinct disadvantages—I got to choose mine first because I was older, and I wanted the one far enough away from everybody that I could get a moment to myself once in a while.

My dad used to practice with his band at our house, and I would pick up their instruments when they were taking breaks. I learned to play the saxophone that way. The drummer for my dad's band was a guy named Max—typical drummer, always a glint in his eye, everything done a little tongue in cheek. I guess he noticed that I liked what he was doing. He gave me my first drum, a marching snare. He showed me the ropes. One day he taught me this thing called *pannenkoeken*, which is just Dutch for "pancakes": a double-stroke roll. And I'm watching him and he goes into this buzz roll and it's *amazing* how he did it. I can't figure it out. "How did you get to *that* from *pannenkoeken*?" I asked him.

"Practice," he told me.

I was so taken by his vibe. He taught me that drums are the *pulse* of the music. Indispensable! We stayed in touch until about three years ago, when he finally passed away.

My dad would take us with him to his gigs sometimes. It was my introduction to the ambiance of a dark club—very sexy, very seductive. The women have on all this perfume, and I see the way they're dancing. It's not a mystery, what you're all there for. Even a kid can figure that one out. The music is the background for the romance of the evening. And I was very drawn to that from an early age. When I was eleven I had my first erotic encounter, with an older woman backstage. (Keep in mind: when you're eleven, everyone is older.) There was so much commotion and carousing; it just kind of happened. It was over sixty years ago, so I don't remember much . . . it's like a vague vision of a doctor's appointment. A very pleasant one.

My dad used to say that as a musician, you can play on anything—you can make music with a chair. It's about communicating a feeling. "It was my mom who really cracked the whip and wanted us to be *proper* musicians; she didn't want us to struggle playing nightclubs like our dad," as Ed once told the guitar journalists Brad Tolinski and Chris Gill. My mom got us into violin next, when I was in fourth grade and Ed was in second, and this became the object of fistfights: guys walking around with little violin cases might as well have been wearing targets. (We gave as good as we got.) Ed and I played violin for about five years, and both of us eventually got into the All City Orchestra, for Pasadena's elite young musicians. That meant we took a bus after school every day to go rehearse. The first of many bus rides to come.

For us, it seemed natural to learn how to play whatever was around. "If you have enough dexterity in your fingers to play keyboards and drums, you can play anything," as my brother put it. We became fluent in a lot of different instruments. After I gave up piano and violin, my mother convinced me to take flamenco guitar lessons. I played saxophone at the first gig Ed and I booked in America, and we decided that Ed would play piano, either Brian or Kevin would be behind their older brother's drum kit, and another guy named Don Ferris would play second sax. It was for our elementary school graduation.

Now, once you make a commitment to playing a venue, you don't play elsewhere in the area for a certain amount of time before the gig, or you lose your draw, right? You get overexposed. But after we signed up to play the graduation, I thought, *Hey, it might be good to have a couple of practice rounds.* So we took another gig and—I couldn't believe it—the school heard about it, came to us, and said, "What are you guys doing? You can't perform somewhere else—you're taking away from the school!"

They took it very seriously. And actually, I was impressed by that professionalism—flattered, even! But we still played both shows; I talked them into it. Because we were not prepared. The difference between playing at home for yourselves and playing in front of your entire school, it's not really a scalable leap. We needed that rehearsal gig. By the time we performed at graduation, we were confident . . . for one thing, having the drum kit onstage made us look real. My dad always told us, people don't come to hear the band, they come to *see* the band. I guess we were fun to watch because after that we were suddenly the most popular guys at elementary school.

We all had shaggy hair like the Beatles, so we called our band the Broken Combs. (That's not such a bad name, but the titles of our songs left something to be desired: "Boogie Booger" was a memorable one.) You have to understand, in our own minds, we were already successful—it was the only way to go.

I remember once we went with my dad to Local 47, the musicians' union, when I was probably ten and Ed was eight, and saw all these supremely talented guys who were treated like dog meat. They were all wearing these worn-out, ill-fitting suits that they'd been sitting on for too long so the rears were all shiny and threadbare. (Because we were short, our eyes were basically at ass level, so we had plenty of time to contemplate those pants while we were standing in line.) I remember distinctly the smell of stale cigarette smoke. That and looking at Ed and going, "We are *never* going to end up here. This is bullshit." We learned to set our sights higher, on things that might or might not work out, but the hell with it: we were going to get there or die trying.

A few years later, when I was thirteen, I had my first professional gig. It was New Year's Eve—a big night for a band like my dad's—and their drummer, Max, had a high-paying gig booked. When the band got offered a last-minute job at the Continental, this club at the Continental bus line stop on Cahuenga Boulevard, my dad said, "You're coming along."

My pops told me, "Keep your head down and nobody will notice you're a kid." It was the first time I was under those blinding spotlights and I was vibratingly uncomfortable behind the drum set when we started playing. I was thinking, *I'm not cutting it. This is not right.* Things like that. *How do I get better?* That was the main thing.

Honestly? I was scared shitless. What if I screwed up? What if I embarrassed him? My dad was a musician: to fail him in this context . . . just the *idea* of his disappointment made me queasy. The essence of being a Van Halen man was at stake: Are you a professional? Can you do what needs to be done under pressure? Will you provide for your family—can they depend on you? Can you *adapt*?

And—most important!—with all of that roiling inside you, can you swing?

Our dad didn't need to verbalize his reverence for music. He transmitted that to us through the way he lived. He had records from every composer that you could possibly imagine, and all these books about them—he knew the history of *all* these people. And that bled into how we saw the world. By the time Ed and I were in sixth grade, we knew all of them and we played all their music with varying degrees of success. "But then do you know what *not* to do?" That's what my dad used to say. He meant, it's not enough that you know how to play. The other half of the coin is you should know what you *can't* do—and don't show people that!

The stuff that excites you early on carries through for the rest of your life. I was listening to Louie Bellson, Hal Blaine—he's unappreciated by the larger public, but Blaine is one of the most influential drummers who ever lived. He was the drummer for the Wrecking Crew and man, he was the guy. He knew it's not about how fast you can play or how many paradiddles you can squeeze in. The space in between, the quiet parts. That's where the magic comes in. That's where the music is happening.

I never really doubted I'd be in a band, and I never doubted it would be with my brother. But we didn't know what kind of music we'd play until the British Invasion made it clear. "We moved to America, we saw *A Hard Day's Night*," said Ed, "and I stopped playing piano." We wanted to rock 'n' roll like our idols: the Beatles and the Dave Clark Five. (You may never have heard of that second band, but back then they were neck and neck with the Beatles, I'm telling you. Songs like "Glad All Over"—that stuff was amazing. We were hooked on that grungy saxophone, and it was an instrument we already knew how to play, so we could imitate their sound.)

We were excited by the wildness and the rebellion of rock. That whole thing with rock 'n' roll being bigger than life? That really appealed to us. It felt like hope. There was a kind of floating negativity at that time—we didn't have an optimistic outlook for the future. The Cuban Missile Crisis happened months after we docked in New York! We were sure we were going to get bombed. Rock 'n' roll made you want to get up and dance; it made you want to twist and shout. It made you feel *better*—and that's what people remember after they see a band: not what you played, but how you made them feel.

We couldn't play what we now considered to be our kind of music on the piano and the violin. "We wanted to rock 'n' roll," Ed told an audience—including me, in the front row—at the Smithsonian in Washington, DC, after they put his guitar in the museum there. "I stopped playing piano for one reason: I was forced to do it and I wasn't allowed to play what I wanted, so it wasn't fun. So I rebelled and bought myself a drum kit." Ed got his heart set on a St. George drum kit that cost a hundred and twenty-five bucks, and I wanted a Teisco Del Rey guitar, which was around the same price. We started a paper route to make money for our instruments; my dad would drive us if it was raining. As this tight-knit immigrant family, we kind of did everything together. And we never stopped working.

For a while Ed and I were going door to door with a can of spray paint and a stencil, offering to repaint people's street numbers on the curb for a modest fee. "My mother and father used to tell Alex and I, 'Get a job, have something to fall back on,'" Ed remembered. "Al has this bright idea, he goes, 'Put this blue overall on.' So we go down to San Marino, which is a real rich section of the South Pasadena area, and Alex would go knock on the doors and say, 'Hi, I'm from San Marino Department of Whatever.' And I'd be sitting out in the car taping up the house number to paint the number on the house, and Al would charge them three bucks, and that's how we made money."

Eventually, with some savings and a loan from our old man, Ed got his drums and I got my guitar. The point was to have a band—I don't think either of us was particularly attached to any one instrument back then. Ed didn't care if I banged around on his drum set and I was happy to let him strum my Teisco. "The only reason why I stopped playing drums was because my brother got better than me, so I said, 'Fuck you, I'll play your guitar!'" Ed once told a journalist.

The first songs we learned were surf-rock classics by the Ventures and the Surfaris—"Pipeline" and "Wipeout," that kind of thing. (I mean, we lived in Southern California: what'd you expect?) We'd listen to Cream records on the turntable at 16 rpm instead of 33, so it was super slow and we could figure out the notes and play along. "My mom always hated what she called 'that high crying noise'—in other words, soloing," Ed said. "She'd always go, 'Why do you have to make that high crying noise?'" My mom was on to something. Ed used the guitar to express his deepest feelings from the very beginning; he *was* crying with it a lot of the time. If our mother didn't like the sound of that wail, can you blame her? It's hard to hear your kid suffer.

When we saw the movie they made about Woodstock, I remember two things. First: no Led Zeppelin?! *WTF?* Second, I was into Michael Shrieve's drum solo when Santana played. Both Ed and I were frustrated because our eyes had to follow the camera's lens—we couldn't see the stuff we were actually interested in. "They had so many close-ups of things but you never got to see the big picture of the bands performing," as Ed put it to Brad Tolinski and Chris Gill, who used to interview him all the time. It got us thinking about image and how you had to harness the attention of the cameraman if you wanted to shape what people experienced of your performance. We saw right then how important that was for a musician, how you couldn't afford to ignore that.

Ed loved Alvin Lee's song "I'm Going Home," which had a wild guitar solo. One day, Ed was messing around with my guitar and out of nowhere he played that solo, note for note—he *nailed* that song. It was brilliant. We were blown away. Nobody else could do that, at least nobody we knew. That was the day we realized it: Ed was a guitar virtuoso.

Fucking A, I thought. *Here, Ed, you play guitar.*

TWO

When we were little, we had this toy gun, a little Mattel shotgun. Ed and I got into it one day over whose turn it was to play with the thing. My dad comes up, grabs the gun, and breaks it in half. He goes, "Here. Now you each have a piece."

It broke my heart. But it showed me: 100 percent of nothing is nothing. My dad, the King Solomon of Pasadena, was remarkable in the way that he would teach us. It was just little tidbits, here and there, and after maybe a couple of years, you'd realize, *Oh, so that's what he meant.* And the most important thing he taught us—with that gun, and in a hundred other ways—was *stick together.*

So, when it became clear that Ed had the gift that he did, I was thinking, *That's getting our foot in the door!* Ed's talent was an asset, not just to me, not just to him. It was an asset to our band, this thing that was bigger than us, that was going to be the vehicle for all of our dreams. Of course, the band was more or less imaginary at this point, but if Ed could play guitar like that, we had something nobody else ever could. I played guitar first and I didn't have that. *This is you, man.* That's how I felt. *Just play, Ed—the rest will take care of itself.*

"All I remember is me going out and throwing papers and he was playing my drums," Ed said at the Smithsonian, motioning toward me, where I was sitting in the front row with his son, Wolfgang. "To watch Al play drums, he wasn't just keeping time, he was making music on the drums. It just came so natural to him, whereas he'll probably say the guitar was just so easy for me—and we're both right." We ended up on the right instruments. "It was destiny," as Ed put it.

I'VE BEEN SOBER FOR DECADES now, but if memory serves, part of the allure of wine is that you're drinking something that's both alive—the juice of a grape, fermenting—and on its way toward death: eventually the stuff will stop aging to perfection and just go off. So in a sense, you're drinking the life cycle. And that faint taste of decay can be kind of bewitching. Along those same lines, part of what made Ed so great wasn't just the way he played a note and brought it to life. The magic was also in the way he'd get the sounds to dissipate, to die. Next time you're listening to him, check it out: the sounds going are as interesting as the sounds coming. I know this sounds like a stretch, but I honestly think Ed was able to convey profound truths about the universe through his music.

"When I found the guitar, I refused to take lessons," Ed said. "This was my real emotional release, and I didn't want to be taught how to approach the instrument." It wasn't like piano, where the Russian teacher would whack his knuckles with a ruler if Ed did something heretical. He was free to use the guitar however it served him. Ed held his pick differently from the way people are taught to—for instance, between his middle finger and thumb . . . which worked out just fine for him, to put it mildly. Leave it to our mother to tell the guitar prodigy that she knows better. "My mom goes, 'You're doing it wrong,'" said Ed. "I'm going, 'Wait a minute: it's music *theory*, not music fact. So don't tell me I'm doing it wrong.'"

One of the things that Ed loved so much about guitar was that suddenly, he had more control over his sound—he had more nuanced ways to express himself because he was now in charge of the strings themselves. "With a guitar you can bend or use vibrato to reach all those microtonal notes and those feelings that fall between the cracks on the piano," is how Ed put it. "There's a touch involved with the piano, but you're not actually touching the strings. So there's an agent between you and the strings—a middleman." Ed could now enjoy an unmediated relationship with his instrument, and he made the most of that.

The strings weren't enough, of course. Ultimately, Ed wanted to mess with the whole guitar. After a few years on my Teisco, he upgraded to a hollow-body Univox Custom twelve-string guitar that had this cool red-and-black sunburst design. He decided he only wanted a six-string, though, so he removed all the upper-octave strings. "That was my very, very first successful attempt at changing something on a guitar that was not up to my liking," he said. It became a way of life.

Eventually, Ed took the Univox to a store called Music for Everyone in Sierra Madre and used the credit toward a gold-top Gibson Les Paul Standard. Naturally, he had his way with that one, too. He didn't like the sound on the single-coil soap-bar pickup, so he took a chisel to the thing. Then he rammed a humbucking pickup in the bridge. Next, he stripped off the gold finish and painted the guitar black. Ed explained, "Since the beginning, everything I picked up off the rack at a music store— even the expensive stuff—did not do what I wanted it to do."

He only liked the way his amp sounded when it was turned all the way up—you know that *Spinal Tap* joke, "These go to eleven"? Ed wanted one that went to twelve. So he tried experimenting with the voltage using a light switch dimmer. Needless to say, he blew out the power at our house.

He tried all different things—stuffing the amp with padding, aiming it at the wall—trying to get the feedback tones he was into without making everybody deaf. Eventually he figured out he could use a Variac variable power supply turned down below 110 volts to overload the vacuum tubes and get those tones at a lower volume, and that was a solution of sorts. "Those amps used to blow like every other gig, and you would have to retube them every other day, but they crank," Ed said. Dave called all of Ed's tweaked creations "Dennis the Menace bits of trouble," and there was that element. Sometimes it was like, *Jesus, Ed, stop fucking around with everything so much and just play already!*

You have to understand, where we grew up, the idea of taking something you'd spent a lot of money on and changing it to suit your own personal whims didn't seem strange. We were surrounded by hot rod culture; people were always souping up their cars with junkyard parts and customizing them with racing stripes and flashy hubcaps and whatnot. We loved cars, but music was our life. Ed wasn't going to spend his precious time and money on whatever crap car we were driving around. He applied all his ingenuity and creativity to tweaking his instruments, so they'd be just a little bit closer to his fantasy.

The sound he wanted was always just out of reach. Ed spent his entire life chasing after it.

NATURALLY, WE GRAVITATED TOWARD OTHER kids who were obsessed with music, and some of them were really important in our lives. There was Dan Scruggs, who got us into the blues and Eric Clapton, when I was probably thirteen. We played with him and another kid, Denis Travis, and called our band the Trojan Rubber Company. (I know: classy.) Denis's dad was a preacher, and very strictly antidrug, but where there's a will, there's a way: We'd make "nuclear tea" before we jammed over there. You get as many tea bags as you can find and steep them for hours on end until the brew is almost black, and man, you get a rush from that stuff when you chug it.

It sounds ridiculous, but it didn't seem that way to us at the time. Honestly, I still respect the impulse. You do whatever you think it takes to create an improved version of yourself—meaning deeper, more articulate, more creative. Every artist, visual or musical, has that itch that can't be scratched to hit some universal vibration . . . it's always just outside your reach, just around the corner, and that's what keeps you going. If you believe drinking the world's strongest cup of tea is going to get you in the state you need to enter to be your most inventive and productive, then go put the kettle on. Bottoms up.

Human beings have always wanted to experience transcendence. Different cultures have gone after it in different ways—whether it's through drumming or dancing, peyote or self-inflicted pain. Kafka (and plenty of Buddhist monks who came before him and since) thought you could get there just by tuning in to the thrum of the universe. "You do not need to leave your room. Remain sitting at your table and listen," he wrote. "Do not even listen, simply wait, be quiet, still and solitary. The world will freely offer itself to you to be unmasked, it has no choice, it will roll in ecstasy at your feet." Every civilization has its own path, but the craving to transcend, that's just part of the human experience.

We started playing music "professionally" when my dad would drag us along to his gigs; that's how we learned how it all worked. He told me early on, play each night like it's your last—but knowing you're probably going to play forever. As in: Give them everything you've got. And then give it to them again tomorrow. That's what he taught us, and that's what he lived by himself.

If there was an opportunity for us to play something, he would put us in. It was never really a planned, conscious effort, but that's how it was: we were a team, and we were always working, striving. I remember a night when Ed and I were playing, and I could see my dad organizing the crowd, passing a hat around. At the end of the gig I asked him, "So, how much did we pull in?" He says, "Seventeen dollars. Here's five for you; here's five for Ed."

"Okay, wait a minute, five and five is ten," I said. "What happened to the other seven?"

"Welcome to the music business," he told me.

I'll never forget that. He could have explained it a million times, and I wouldn't have gotten it: *That's how this works.* You learn much better by actually experiencing something than you do just hearing about it. It was extremely lucky for Ed and for me that we had a whole education in the life of a musician before we were even professional musicians.

It was definitely starting to seep into my identity, though—being a musician, and more specifically being a drummer. The dancers in the clubs where my dad played were, for the most part, just people off the street who were into ballroom dancing. But there were also some semiprofessional folks, and when you watched them, you learned when to kick it up a notch as a drummer. You could tell where to give them a little boost, you know?

As I started to work more and more with my dad, people would come and tell me, "We've never had a drummer who can make us dance like this." I don't know if it was actually true or not, but I remember that vividly, hearing that compliment. My distinct feeling afterward was, *Uh-oh: now I've got to do it every time.*

Sometimes my dad would get these gigs at wealthier events for golfers and that kind of thing. I remember one at this place called La Mirada country club. He said, "Bring your drums, and, Ed, get your guitar and your amp." My mom came, too. We got there and everything was alarmingly professional. This wasn't just some garage where we were playing—suddenly we were playing in a real, you know, *venue*. We got a little nervous.

The dinner was steak and baked potato. Well, we'd never seen that before—we didn't eat meat that way. We boiled it, and we cooked it to death so it was soft and it fell apart. We sat there struggling, trying to saw the steak into pieces, until one of us said to hell with it. My mom put the steaks in her purse, and we took all that meat home to cook it our way.

Ed probably felt a little awkward playing with my dad's band because the guitar parts were much more difficult than the drums. For me it was straightforward: if you could swing, you could maintain. Didn't matter what the song was, the ins and outs of the setups and all that. Keep time, and swing the band. (My dad used to say, "If anyone asks what 'swing' is, they'll never get it." You can't define it. But you'll know it when you feel it!) It's not that drums are an easier instrument to play; there's just less to remember. For a guitarist, on some of those old standards, you need a chart to keep track of where all the chords are just to make it through the night.

When you're playing your best, sometimes you start *thinking* about it, and then you completely lose your flow. So what did we do to get out of our heads?

We drank.

THREE

My teachers all gave up on me
No matter what they say, I disagree
And when I need something to soothe my soul
I listen to too much rock 'n' roll

—*Van Halen, "Fools"*

I had my first drink when I was six—schnapps; my dad gave it to me. He didn't give me a pacifier; to placate me he gave me a tobacco pipe. You have to understand, in postwar Holland, everybody around us was smoking and drinking. In Northern Europe, you have alcohol with ceremony, you have alcohol in church, you have alcohol when you sit down to dinner. You need alcohol just to make it through the winter—and that winter goes on forever.

People there will tell you, "Yeah, but we only have one or two." Well, one or two never did it for me. Give me ten.

I was young when I first realized that alcohol had that effect on me—that it lifted my spirits like nothing else. For people whose bodies react to alcohol the way mine does, it's like you've gone back to the womb. Everything is warm and fuzzy, no matter where you happen to be. Even as a kid I knew that anything that could make me feel that good . . . well, you're going to have a problem somewhere down the line.

I remember a girlfriend said to me once, "Do you like yourself better when you drink?" I told her, "No, but I like you better."

It's a good comeback, but the truth is I liked *everything* better.

We were taught that drinking was just what you did: to celebrate, to party, to take the edge off, to steel yourself when the shit hit the fan. When Ed was twelve, my cousin's German shepherd jumped through our screen door and sank his teeth into my brother's thigh. My dad's prescription was to give him a cigarette and a shot of vodka. (Dogs *hated* Ed; they were always going after him. Maybe because he exuded so much vulnerability, or who the hell knows. Whatever the reason, it happened all the time. I remember once going over to visit our friend Julio. We'd just walked in the door, I was looking around, and two minutes later I heard this yelling and screaming: it was Ed being chased down the street by a beagle. Funniest thing I've ever seen.)

"I remember when my dad got me into drinking and smoking when I was twelve: I was nervous, so he said to me, 'Here, have a shot of vodka.' Boom. I wasn't nervous anymore," Ed said. "I don't drink for the taste of it," he continued. "I drink to get a fucking buzz! I like to get drunk. I really do."

Alcohol was definitely a problem in our family. I remember going to visit my dad when they'd thrown him in the military hospital to dry out before we left Holland. I didn't understand what was happening at the time. All I knew was, it's your pops; you go see him. I vividly remember a smell of ether, and that the place was extremely low-tech—it looked like those pictures you see of Russian orphanages, just row after row of sterile cots. I pretended like nothing was wrong or out of the ordinary. My mother didn't explain or really say much of anything about where we were or what we were doing there, so I just looked out the window the whole time, hoping he wasn't too sick. At that time, you really didn't question your parents. They knew everything, and, most of all, they *ruled* everything, so you just went along with whatever they came up with.

Here's a good example of what I mean. This is the weirdest thing, but at home, my mom would tell me to knock my dad out if she felt he was getting out of line, too drunk and rowdy, hollering. He was certainly never violent—*she* would start hitting *him*. Ed was completely useless when it came to this stuff; he just left me to handle it. "My mom would be chasing my dad with a pan and slamming him on the head," Ed said. "To escape from that I would play the piano or hide in my room playing guitar." Meanwhile, I'd be watching things unravel—and managing the situation on my own. *Thanks a lot, Ed!*

One of the things I learned in the course of my upbringing was that you really have to be able to pivot, you really have to be able to maneuver, because at any given moment, maybe your dad is right—but now maybe your mom is right—and you're stuck in this weird turmoil, and you have to adapt, fast.

Things would escalate. And my dad *was* out of line, sometimes. And if your mother tells you to do something, when you're a kid, you just do it. So I had to go through with it. I hit him on the head with a glass quart bottle of Miller beer.

It was like something you'd see on *I Love Lucy*. But when it hit, it didn't shatter like things do on TV. I could actually feel it going into my father's soft skull tissue. And then he went down. It was a very, very uncomfortable feeling. I was just really sad, you know, *This is my father, why am I doing this?* That and, *Hey, Ed! How about a little help?*

We never talked about it. I hope he forgives me. Probably, he didn't remember. Or maybe my father thought he deserved it.

WE WERE A PHYSICAL FAMILY. "I'm going to kick your ass" was almost a term of endearment to us. My father had a blackjack he kept under the stairs, and he was always threatening that if we did this or that he'd beat the shit out of us with that thing. He never actually did; the worst that would happen is he'd give us a smack if we were out of hand. Ed and I played rough—like most brothers. Sometimes, when my dad wanted to sit down and have a quiet dinner after a long day—which usually followed a long night—he would get fed up with me and Ed creating havoc, laughing uncontrollably, running around the table, and one of us would get whacked.

My mom couldn't whack; she was too small. Her thing was to hit your hand with a wooden spoon. Once, she did it so hard my whole thumbnail fell off afterward.

It was a different era. Corporal punishment was the norm. And the sickest part is that they convinced us we had it coming!

Ed took that kind of thing harder than I did, more personally. "Whenever I didn't practice or when I started playing guitar, my mom used to call me a 'nothing-nut, just like your father.' When you grow up that way, it's not conducive for self-esteem," Ed said. *Nietsnut* is what my mom used to shout at him; it's a Dutch way of calling someone a nobody. I never took that kind of thing seriously. My mom was just trying to discipline and motivate us. But I guess Ed took it in at face value and always felt like he had something to prove . . . even long after he'd shown the world he was the furthest thing from a nobody.

Ed and I, like all brothers, or at least all the brothers I know, beat on each other whenever we had the chance. I still have a scar on my face from where Ed cut me with a bamboo "sword" when we were back in Holland. What happened was that one morning, my mom had a cup of coffee that she put down on the washing machine. (The apartment was very small—everything was within arm's reach no matter where you stuck it.) Ed grabbed at something and his hand hit the saucer and the boiling-hot coffee spilled on him; he had second- and third-degree burns all over his body. My parents rushed him to the hospital, where they wrapped him in bandages like a mummy, and they had all these little sort of bamboo sticks strategically placed to keep the bandages from adhering to his blisters. It wasn't long before we were using those bamboo sticks for fencing practice.

There were very few things that we did apart. The assumption was that anything I was doing he was doing, and vice versa, especially when it came to music. Any deviation from that was unpleasant.

Ed felt left out when I would go and work with my father and he wasn't invited because he was still a kid. Ed being the second born, he was always kind of vying for Dad's attention. Of course, I was thinking, *Be my guest, Ed: you go and do all this shit instead of me!* I didn't know if I *wanted* to be working all the time at eleven, twelve years of age. But to Ed it looked like we had something between us that he didn't get in on. I guess that's just how it is with siblings.

Don't get me wrong: I was as attached to Ed as he was to me. I have some old video of Ed playing with another guy onstage at his graduation from elementary school, and it still pisses me off to watch it. (Just kidding.) (Sort of.) Granted, the reason *I* couldn't play with Ed that day is that I was in the seventh or eighth grade by then, and this was an elementary school thing. So I ended up being the roadie, thinking: *I'm going to keep an eye on this.* I was carrying that amp, literally keeping Ed tethered.

Then there was a band that rehearsed in a washing machine store in Monrovia—they really went after Ed. We went to see them; I must have been at least sixteen because I drove us there. Their bait was that they had a record deal. And you remember—I certainly did—my dad saying, *Don't fight over the gun,* so to speak. Once you get your foot in the door, then you can maneuver. *If they have a record deal, then this could be good for us. (And their drummer will be gone before you know it.)* But they were so bad it didn't matter. Their big song was called "Dear Diary," for Christ's sake.

We had our minds made up about what we wanted to be: Cream. I would show off by playing my idol Ginger Baker's drum solo from the song "Toad"; Ed would listen to Clapton for hours and study what he was doing. "Hendrix I like, but I was never into him like I was Clapton," Ed told *Guitar World* in 1978. "Clapton, man. I know every fucking solo he ever played, note for note, still to this day."

The first concert we ever saw was Clapton with Derek and the Dominos when they played the Pasadena Civic Auditorium in 1970. A friend of Ed's had won the tickets from a local radio station and handed them over because he knew Clapton was Ed's idea of God. We were in the sixth row but Ed brought *binoculars* so he could see every detail of what Clapton was doing.

But he was disappointed. He talked about it to a journalist decades later: "To be honest with you, I was expecting something more powerful. If I would've seen Cream, I probably would've been blown away because that's the era of Clapton that I really loved." Still, we tried to sneak backstage after the gig so we'd get to see Clapton walk by. Didn't happen; he probably split before we got anywhere close. "But we did get to meet the tambourine player," Ed remembered. "Al and I cracked up because the guy actually had a little flight case for his tambourine."

We were dying about it at the time. But I get it now. Musicians get attached to their instruments. "You have to be emotionally and spiritually connected to your instrument," as Ed said. "A guitar is a very personal extension of the person playing it." I feel the same way. To me, playing drums—viciously attacking something—has been an outlet and a means of communication; I'd be in a lot of trouble if I'd never found the drums. Your instrument, it's not a living thing, but you still have a relationship with it, an intimacy, and if anything were to happen to it you'd grieve it as a real loss.

The harshest punishment my mother ever came up with for Ed was to lock up his guitar to prevent him from practicing.

"I HATED FOLLOWING YOU IN school," Ed told me many times. There were two problems: my grades were good (at least when I tried), *and* I was a troublemaker.

In terms of the first thing, I started out as a straight-A student. I think it was just a freak thing, but they tested me and I did well. I wish they hadn't—it caused me nothing but grief, and I don't think it means *anything*. But my mom did. She took it to heart, and the next thing you knew, you had this little four-foot-tall Indonesian woman coming into the school, clearly out of her element, antagonizing all the teachers. She wanted me in the gifted program, but I had no interest in being there. Because I didn't see any pretty girls in that class! That shows you where my—supposedly intelligent—head was at.

My mom was focused on how to get ahead in a new country and she had very particular ideas about what that looked like. "Why can't you do IBM?" she would say. She was thinking big, and she had a delusion that my supposedly superior intellect was going to get us somewhere. I didn't want to spend my life staring at computer screens. I wanted to bang on things! Hard!

I guess Ed always felt like he was unintelligent. I don't know what he was talking about; I never felt smarter than him or anything like that. Like I've said, he was sensitive. One shitty teacher probably called him dumb one time, and he could never let it go.

Ed was right, though, that teachers would get him in their class and have the attitude, "Here we go, another Van Halen." Because I kind of rebelled against my mother's expectations, academically speaking, and pretty soon I was seen as an instigator. I had this biology teacher, Mrs. Walker, who had a little clicker, and if she wanted us to pay attention, she'd click it at us like we were a bunch of animals. It just seemed really disrespectful. I felt like, *Hey, I've got hair growing out of my face, lady—and take a look at what's going on with my body. Don't treat me like a child.* So I bought clickers for everyone in my class and the next time she pulled hers out to click at us, we all clicked right back. If there's one thing I've never been able to tolerate, it's unearned, arbitrary authority.

I got in a physical fight with my high school shop teacher, Mr. Carlson. You see, we had this off-campus paper called the *Bull Sheet*, and it was all people's opinions on everything going on in school. You weren't allowed to be anonymous: if you want to say some shit, okay, go ahead, but you have to sign your name to it and take responsibility. It was the second-to-last day of high school, and I had the *Bull Sheet*. Mr. Carlson comes up to me and says, "Give me that." I said, "No way." So he got pushy and I pushed back. My feeling was, *There's no hope for me anyway; I have to go to Vietnam soon.* So I took a swing at Mr. Carlson and ended up in the principal's office. I walk in and Mr. Charles—our first Black principal, incidentally—looks at me and shakes his head. He says, "Just give him the fucking piece of paper"—he used that exact language—"and I'll graduate you."

I took the deal. Mr. Charles didn't mention that he was going to award me a D-minus average. But I squeaked by, which was more than a lot of my friends could say. Academically, Ed and my crowd, we just had no direction; we were not really there to get an education. You knew you weren't going to go to college; you couldn't afford it. And I'd already decided, if they called me up to go to Vietnam, I was going to go—this country took us in. It never happened, though, because my draft number was too high. By *one*.

I guess when you follow somebody else, it makes it tough. Ed once told *Guitar World*, "I used to sit on the edge of my bed with a six-pack of Schlitz Malt talls. My brother would go out at 7 p.m. to party and get laid, and when he'd come back at 3 a.m., I'd be sitting in the same place, playing guitar." Now, it's true Ed spent an unbelievable amount of time noodling with his guitar by himself—and that was on top of the endless hours we spent jamming together. He literally couldn't get enough of it. "When I first picked up the guitar there was no message from God or anything," he continued in that interview. "Some things were easy and some things were hard. But I didn't even think about whether it was easy or hard; it was something I wanted to do, to have fun and feel good about doing it. Whether it took me a week to learn half a song or one day to learn five songs, I never thought of it that way." He was addicted to his instrument and God knows he put in the time making his guitar gently weep. But I wouldn't exactly say I was the only one interested in partying and playing the field.

Ed got into his own trouble. He was expelled from our school system when he was sixteen or seventeen after he got busted for possession—of a joint, but that was enough. It was a felony offense, and we weren't citizens yet, so my parents were briefly convinced we were going to get kicked out of the country. My dad was nonchalant as always: "Well, maybe we'll move to Scotland." I, on the other hand, went and beat up the guy who ratted Ed out.

I felt like I *had* to—like it was my responsibility, and I needed to do the right thing for my little brother. It was drilled into my head from the time we were very young children that looking out for Ed, protecting him, was part of my job description. Once we were adults, I gave him plenty of opportunities to take care of me, and he always did. I'm grateful for it. But as kids, in our family—which was old-world and old-school, like I've said—the role I was assigned was very clear. Your little brother's in trouble? Take care of it. Your brother got busted for pot? Take the rap, find the right person to talk to, do whatever the hell you have to do, but figure out a way to fix it. And I tried to, for sixty-five years. If it were up to me, I'd still be trying.

The entire school watched me kick the ass of the kid who'd supposedly told on Ed. Eventually, the cops came and took me in, and I got a couple years of probation for it. But that's not the bad part. I beat up the wrong guy.

I felt truly awful about that—I knew how wrong it was. Karma got me back. A few months later I was hanging out in the park and a group of seven or eight guys came and beat the living crap out of me with golf clubs. Ed saw the whole thing from a distance, but he had no idea I was at the bottom of the pile. These were guys who had nothing to do with the poor schmuck at school I'd pummeled—there was no relationship between the two beatings, except in my mind, where it seemed like I'd gotten what I had coming to me.

Ed ended up having to go to a place called continuation education, where you're not going to learn anything except how to continue doing the stuff that got you there in the first place. He was always inclined toward rebellion; there's a reason rock 'n' roll spoke to him. He loved "It's My Life" by the Animals—you know, "It's my life and I'll do what I want." That and "We Gotta Get Out of This Place," another Animals song about resisting the status quo. "Emotionally, I just dug those lyrics," Ed once told a journalist. They articulated his dominant feelings at the time.

You can imagine that none of this delighted my mother, who'd had dreams of producing a pair of respectable young men. She would yell and scream at us, or sometimes just shake her head. Ed and I naturally gravitated toward the misfits—we were not in the tennis-racket-carrying crowd. Pasadena was different back then; it wasn't the homogeneous, manicured suburb it is today. We came from a mixed neighborhood—we had some Native American kids, some Hispanic, some Black—where people fought and the environment was scrappy. The truth is, of the guys I hung around with in high school, besides me, only one has managed to stay alive.

In the environment where I grew up, men were expected to behave in certain ways. You were supposed to stand up for yourself and your family. You were supposed to be strong, tough, and—in a nonacademic way, at least—responsible. You could be a hard-drinking musician, but you had to have a *different* kind of discipline: you had to practice, you had to provide, and you had to work your ass off.

And I did. As a teenager, besides getting through high school, I was already taking extra classes at this electrician school, and I had two or three different jobs because we needed the money, plus I was trying to get the band going, and I needed *some* time for my newfound interests in drinking, drugs, and girls. I was stretched thin! There were all these different colliding demands and issues, and I really felt like I was doing my duty—pulling my weight and then some. Maybe that's why one day, when I got home from school and my dad came up from behind and whacked me upside the head because he thought I'd been cutting class, I clocked him.

Sure, it was a semiautomatic reaction. But I was also in an instant, affronted rage, accelerated by testosterone and adrenaline, thinking, *I* was *at school, who told you I wasn't?* (Probably my mother.) So I knocked out my own father. And I have regretted it every day since.

It's probably the one thing I've done that bothers me the most, that I feel the most ashamed of. He wrongly accused me of a small violation of our family code of honor, and I responded with the biggest violation of it imaginable. In all the time that we worked together, driving to these gigs in the middle of nowhere, we never talked about it. Really, my father and I barely talked at all for a year or two after that incident. We just drank together. Often, on those long drives home from playing music at some club, we were both drunk as a skunk and could barely see the road.

Like I said, Ed felt left out of all that.

FOUR

I hope that within the next 5 or 6 years I reach my goal
as a rock star. It might sound funny but that's what I
want. Many bands nowadays depend more or less on
their freaky show but I would like to be respected more
for my music than for a show. I'll do whatever I have to,
to become a rock star.

*—Edward Van Halen, in a high school paper about his aspirations for the
future, November 21, 1963*

You are very talented, but if you are as shy onstage as
you are in class, it will be very difficult for you to make
it as a performer.

—His teacher's response

I remember going to see Zeppelin with Ed when I was maybe
sixteen at the Forum and it was almost a religious experience
for us. The smell of pot was so potent in there it was like we

were inside a bong. And the sound was just incredible. The downside was that they didn't play anything the way it was on the record, but just the sheer, raw nakedness of it, the wall of sound coming at us . . . It was completely overpowering. Those guys could have played "Happy Birthday" and it would have come out a rock 'n' roll song—they were just so distinct! And it was exciting being surrounded by tons of other young people who loved them (almost) as much as we did. And who were just dying to blow the roof off.

It was a very vibrant, fertile music scene we were aspiring to enter, because of the energy, the vibe, not only the sound. Everybody had their own individual look, from Zeppelin and the Beatles to T. Rex and the Doobie Brothers. When my dad came home from work on weekends, we would sit around the TV watching *Don Kirshner's Rock Concert* or *The Midnight Special*. He would give a little running commentary, just simple things. I remember once we were watching Liberace, and my father said, "You see the candelabra?" And that was all he said. But I knew what he meant: *What is your visual reference that makes you different from anybody else?* At that point, Ed and I were just a couple of teenagers with long hair in T-shirts and cords. There was room for improvement.

It wasn't just our look that needed work, though. Ed *was* shy; his teacher was right. "Everybody goes through their teens getting fucked around by a chick or not fitting in with the jocks at school. I just basically locked my room for four years," he once said. (Which was a stretch: What "lock," Ed? What "room"?! Ed never let the truth get in the way of a good story when he was giving an interview. But you get the idea.) He was the lead singer of our band, but he was a musical prodigy, not a front man. And he didn't want to put on a freaky show.

But *somebody* had to. People don't come to hear a band just because of the music. They want to be transported. They want permission to go wild and release their inhibitions. And you're there to lead the charge. "I'm actually a shy, nervous person," Ed told *Rolling Stone* in '98. Like I said: not a born front man. "I used to sing and play lead . . . and I couldn't stand it." Ed was the farthest thing from an extrovert—his primary relationship was with his guitar.

Some of that was his personality, but some of it had to do with the fact that English was our second language—it didn't just flow naturally for us the way a mother tongue does. So chatting up the crowd was a weak spot, and so were lyrics. We did try to write them for a while: we'd take a Rod McKuen poem and then kind of disassemble it and put it back together and pair it with a two-note lick. I can still remember one: "I talked to the mailman / His shoes were tied / The dog was not eating his lemon midnight."

What the hell does that mean? I have no idea. This is the era of "In the white room, with black curtains." We were into stream of consciousness. Or to put it another way, nonsense—just Beat nonsense. Lyrics, language, poetry . . . it really wasn't where we were at. But if you know what you're missing, then you can find a way to supply it.

ED AND I DECIDED THAT no decent band could be without a manager, so we enlisted the help of a loudmouthed punk kid, who set up a gig for us playing at what has become an infamous party at a park in Pasadena. Ed and I get there first—we always get there first, to suss the place out, check the power supply, see what the lighting is like. Well, there was nothing to see: no stage, no lights. Nothing.

The liaison for the park shows up and he says, "Hey, man, where's the stage gear?" Typical scenario in the infancy of modern rock concerts. "Our manager told me you'd have it!" I hollered. Our manager was mistaken. Well, no stage, no play. So Ed and I went to get a couple drinks.

A few hours later, we went back to the park. Another local band called Red Ball Jet was up. Man, were they *horrible*, at least to our way of thinking. The music was just nondescript. And what were they doing playing *our* gig? Ed and I were egging each other on: Who did they think they were? How was there suddenly a stage?

Anyway, one thing led to another, and I don't know why, but I threw a bottle at them. Not to hurt anybody, just to say, *Hey, we'll take a little of that attention over here!* That kind of stopped the music, and Ed and I made our way up there to say hi to the Komora brothers, Miles and Mark, who played bass and guitar in that band and who we knew from around town. We just wanted to ask them what the hell happened that they'd ended up playing a gig we'd booked. They were really nice guys. But somehow people started pushing and shoving, and before you knew it, the texture and the color and the flavor of the whole deal turned ugly. Somebody pulled a knife. A mini riot broke out.

That was my introduction to Red Ball Jet and their singer, Dave Roth.

In my mind, I was maybe sixteen when I threw that bottle and years went by before Dave ended up auditioning for Ed and me. But that chronology doesn't add up. Time passes differently when you're a teenager, stretching out over the slog that is high school.

It must have been a matter of months, not years. What I know for sure is that from then on, we would see Dave around, always cruising the periphery. We'd run into him at the temple—we were playing, Dave was praying, I always used to say, because Dave's Jewish. The temple was a sort of hub of culture in our area, and they were kind enough to let us rehearse there, so we'd play at their dances and see Dave there, and at backyard parties around Pasadena. And Dave would see us.

Looking at the old mimeographed flyers we would hand out all over Pasadena, the addresses of the parties form a map of my teenage memories—Hamilton Park, Huntington Drive, Colorado Boulevard, Arden Road. If we got to the party and our extension cords couldn't reach the house, we'd set up a generator. It was DIY to the max. "Backyard parties developed into an art form," Dave wrote in his book *Crazy from the Heat*. "Well over two hundred people would show up. This was right about the time, going to one of these parties, that I first saw the Van Halens. It's the brother and the brother, you know, the guitar player and the drummer, with the bass player, doing note for note, *verbatim* renditions of The Who, *Live at Leeds*, or Deep Purple, 'Smoke on the Water,' or shit from Woodstock, when Alvin Lee comes out and plays 'Goin' Home' faster than any known human being on earth, or at least up until that time—Edward could do *that* lick. You know, it was *amazing* stuff." Dave's band was nowhere near as good as ours musically. "There was no signature sound to it," as he put it. "But we had a helluva show. 'Cause I was already Diamond Dave."

He got into the David Bowie thing early. Plaid shirts and corduroys were not the way to go, and Dave figured that out before we did. "During their set, the Van Halens stood around like the guys in Nirvana," in Dave's recollection. (In our defense:

Nirvana was a great band! And extremely successful.) "They wore Levi cords with the boxer shorts stickin' out and a T-shirt, and just sort of stood there, but their music was spectacular."

Well, music ain't enough. As Dave likes to say, "People need to know where to look." He'd started doing solo gigs at a folk music club called the Ice House, and he stuck out like a sore thumb, wearing a tuxedo shirt all the way open, when everyone else there was still in tie-dye and dashikis. Dave had a hairy chest at a very young age, so he *always* had his shirt open, picking the fleas out, so to speak. "They weren't getting the shows in the bars. They couldn't understand why," Dave said. "I explained it to them one day: 'It's because you play all twenty minutes of 'I'm So Glad' by Cream, complete with drum solo, live, note for note, and it's very impressive, but you can't dance to it.' That's not 'Excuse me, do you come here often?' music."

Dave was a hyperactive kid who'd been stuck in leg braces until he was four years old . . . I've never completely understood what they were fixing but they must have done something right, because by the time we got our hands on him he could really use those legs onstage. He'd always been desperate for an audience. "It was never about the music for him, it was about the show," my brother once said about Dave circa Red Ball Jet. "He was like an emcee, a clown. He was great at what he did."

Dave had already moved around all over the country when we first met him. He was born in Bloomington, Indiana, where his dad went to medical school to become an ophthalmologist. After Dr. Roth graduated, they lived for a while out in the Midwestern countryside on a horse ranch. (I own one myself now, because my wife, Stine, does competitive dressage all over the country. I don't get on the horses and ride, but I like being around them and spending time out at the ranch, where it's peaceful and bucolic. I get the appeal.) Dave and his sisters, Allison and Lisa, moved with their folks to Brookline, Massachusetts—a fancy suburb of Boston—next, before they made the final move west to California.

Dave didn't fit in anywhere; the guy was just too out-there. They started giving him clinical treatment for hyperactivity when he was nine because he was so wired and he'd never shut up. He was always doing handstands and showing off; he was obsessed with Bugs Bunny. His parents called his dinnertime shtick "monkey hour." When he was seven, Dave's dad took him to see *Some Like It Hot*. (You remember the old Billy Wilder movie? The one where Jack Lemmon and Tony Curtis dress up as women and pal around with Marilyn Monroe?) And from then on, "life turned into an ongoing quest to be in that movie, just somewhere in that movie," Dave told *Rolling Stone* years later. He really liked cartoons; I think the world looked like one to him.

He was entertaining. Most of the musicians Ed and I went to school with never understood: you're *there* to entertain. My dad always told us, if you don't do that, you'll just end up playing for other musicians. And what's the point of that? Ninety-nine percent of the people you play for are not musicians, so stop catering to them. Cater to the *public*—that's a whole different enchilada. So when Dave approached us about jamming, we were up for it.

It did not go well. We'd agreed to play Johnny Winter's tune "Still Alive and Well." But Dave couldn't get the words out on the beat—Ed and I were finished playing before Dave had even started singing. I'm exaggerating, but only a little: timing was not his forte. My brother put it less delicately: "It was terrible. He couldn't sing." We were young and inflexible, so we told Dave thanks but no thanks, it wasn't a good fit. It was all very polite and professional, and we were friendly when we'd see each other around with the Komora brothers at backyard parties in Pasadena.

We said yes to every imaginable gig. We played *constantly*. First of all, it was all we wanted to do, and second, you have to remember Steve Winwood was only sixteen when he released his first single. As far as Ed and I were concerned, we were falling behind. We had changed our name from the Broken Combs to Genesis, which we thought was much more adult and professional. Unfortunately, we discovered that there was already a British band with that name, and they were a hell of a lot farther along than we were: they already had a record out. We decided we would call ourselves Mammoth, instead—*that's* how big we were going to be.

We didn't have a PA system, though, and we kept finding ourselves in situations where we had to borrow one, often from David Roth. We would always give him five or ten bucks for the use of his equipment. It got to the point where I said to Ed, "Let's play with him again. If he was in the band we'd save a fortune."

This time, we went to Dave's house. He sang the blues song "Ice Cream Man" (and he hasn't stopped singing it since. HA!). Ed hadn't heard it before, and neither had I, so we assumed Dave had written it himself. I thought, *Ed, not in a hundred million years could we write lyrics that good.*

And Dave could *talk*. He was just yakking and yakking about anything and everything, and he can be very charming, very persuasive. They had a bar in that house and there was a suit of armor on the counter with a bottle of whiskey inside the chest. Ed and I kept sneaking over to take little nips from it every time we pretended to go use the bathroom. That made everything Dave was saying that much more interesting.

In terms of his singing, he had no sense of time, but he had an interesting drawl. He was totally unfamiliar with our kind of music. He loved Louis Prima. He desperately wanted to be Al Jolson or James Brown. "The first records that I imitated were Al Jolson—getting down on one knee, you know, with the white gloves, singing, as well as dancing—the idea of entertaining," Dave wrote. "Jolson was the first one to really construct a whole show with wardrobe, dancers, his own lights, his own sound, his own orchestra, and take it on the road." Dave's innate fascination with showmanship, his desire to attract as much attention to himself as humanly possible, was everything we were missing. "It was only later, in hippie years, that the idea of being an entertainer was somehow not cool," Dave continued. "You had to be positively somnambulant, just sort of stand around, catatonic, and jam."

Look, Ed and I had a lot of energy and, probably even then, a certain amount of stage presence. We were far from catatonic. But onstage, we *did* just sort of stand around and jam. Ed told an interviewer, "My brother used to throw drumsticks at me: 'Move, move, jump around!'" Sounds about right.

We were musicians; we weren't about to start dancing and getting down on one knee and wearing white gloves. (At least not until the "Hot for Teacher" video. HA!) And it's not like Ed loved singing. "I would kind of do a Kurt Cobain; after five songs and three beers my voice would be gone," he said. "I would just scream it out."

We knew enough to know that a guy like Dave with his ego and charisma would give us more space to be who *we* really were. The audience could watch Dave while they listened to us play. He knew that was his role, and he liked it. Years later, he described his contribution to Van Halen like so: "I look towards making a show. It's showbiz, it's Broadway, it's tinsel, it's glamour town, it's Hollywood, the lines, Auntie Mame, *Bali Ha'i is calling!* Boom." Yeah. That was not what Ed and I were bringing to the table.

On the one hand I thought his choice of music was bass ackward. But then I also thought if you took our influences and his and put them together, it would make something really different . . . a kind of soup with an interesting mix of ingredients, layers of flavors, that might taste like nothing you'd ever had before. Plus, Dave had the same tenacity and work ethic that we did, and that's extremely rare. And he had that PA system.

Dave convinced me he should be in the band, then I convinced Ed. Ed never would have gotten together with Dave if I hadn't pushed. I was the older brother, and I was the one who convinced him that this was what we should do. So it's my fault! I figured if Dave could convince me he should be in the band, he'd be able to convince just about anyone of anything. If there are five people vying for one seat, who's going to get the job? The loudest, most obnoxious, aggressive motherfucker on the planet. Dave, you've got the job!

"They consented begrudgingly," is how Dave remembers it. "What's more, they didn't have to pay me rent for the PA system anymore. It's what, in the business, is called 'an inducement.'"

What I remember is that after we told Dave he was in, he said, "Okay, great. But you guys have to dress better."

WE ALWAYS HAD DAY JOBS. After the paper route, Ed started moving pianos and organs for a music store in Pasadena called Berry & Grassmueck. That was where he eventually stumbled on a Marshall stack—a hundred-watt amplifier head and two speaker cabinets—that had been used as the house amp at the Rose Palace, this giant cement building in Pasadena where they built the floats for the Rose Parade and sometimes had concerts. Jimi Hendrix played there—through *that* amp.

In general, Marshalls were hard to come by, plus they were the preferred amp of Ed's favorite guitar players: Clapton used a Marshall; so did Jimmy Page. "I had never seen a Marshall before except in pictures," Ed said. "I told them I didn't care how long I had to work there, but I wanted that amp. All I cared about was that it was a Marshall." Ed bought it with his employee discount and spent years hauling pianos around to pay it off.

I started working in a machine shop the day after I graduated from high school . . . it was like I walked straight out of school into that shop. Every malcontent and pervert you can imagine was employed alongside me, along with some real hardworking immigrant family guys. I had a blast for a while, but I almost lost a finger.

I worked in the milling department, and I had the biggest machine there (of course). One day, I'm messing around with this massive magnetic plate, and the thing flies off. My finger goes through the machine, and then it's hanging by a thread. They rushed me to the hospital and sewed me back up. I still have weird numbness in that finger; it's a very strange feeling. (It accounts for the unique snare sound I get . . . that finger is like deadweight and it functions as a damper, kills the overtones.) The only reason the machine didn't chop through the bone is because it was a grinding stone and not a blade that got me. Had it been a blade, my whole life would have been different.

My father lost a finger of his own—or the end of it, anyway—in the early seventies. One night at about one thirty in the morning I woke up to the sound of him yelling and screaming and kicking the door. When I opened it, he was standing there shouting and holding up a finger that was missing about a third with blood spurting out from where the tip used to be. What had happened was that the neighbor across the alley had parked his trailer in such a way that my dad couldn't back into our driveway. The thing was resting on a block of wood, and when Dad went to move the trailer, he hadn't realized how much weight there was on that base. The trailer came crashing down on his hand, and off popped the end of his finger. I jumped in the car with him and rushed him to the hospital, where I found out that as a foreigner with no insurance, you're not exactly a priority. They told us to go to a different hospital, in downtown LA, about a half an hour away. So there I am blazing down the Pasadena Freeway with my father in the wee hours of the morning—and he was in agony. When we finally got to the other hospital, all they did was put a Band-Aid on him! The next morning, I found the tip of his finger on the ground next to the trailer. His fingernail was still on it, and there were ants crawling all over it. I put the thing in a little jar of alcohol, and we kept it in the closet for the next ten years, where Ed and I would go look at it from time to time.

Anyway. There wasn't a proper guard on my machine at the shop, and I didn't realize this after the accident, but they were very afraid I was going to sue them. That was never going to happen, though, because my cousin was the manager, and I'm not going to screw him over. He gave me the job, right?

But what I could do is say, "I'm out of here." I only got paid a dollar an hour! I wasn't putting any of my fingers in the closet next to Dad's.

I bought my first proper drum kit once I got out of the machine shop. It was a Ludwig, and it cost a thousand bucks. I still remember walking into the Village Music Store in Sierra Madre. Mr. Shepherd, the proprietor, was a really nice guy, and I paid him in the one-dollar bills I'd made at the shop. That stack of cash directly represented a thousand hours of my work, a thousand hours of my life, and he understood that.

I still have that drum kit. We've had some good times together.

DAVE HAD A FRIEND, LIZ, who said we could use her garage to rehearse—for free! It was very generous of her, and we were grateful to have the space; I taught her little son how to play drums. ("He would go into the garage while the band was practicing and for some reason he liked to curl up in the biggest drum and stay there while the band was playing," she recalled. "Alex, unlike many drummers, did not use pillows or blankets to muffle that big drum." No way! I'm not trying to put you to sleep with my drums, I'm trying to get you up on your feet!) The only problem was that her house was in a sketchy neighborhood, so we had to break down all our equipment every night after we finished and then bring it back to set up the next day; if we left it overnight, it would have gotten stolen.

For a little while we had a keyboard player in the band, mostly because he came with a dance studio his family owned, which they allowed us to use for rehearsal. He had perfect pitch but no common sense! Eventually we had to part ways.

We ended up rehearsing in Dave's basement—which I thought was a bad idea. He's got the power now; you're not going to tell him, "This isn't working, man," after his family has bent over backward to allow us to play there. Not that the space was so fantastic: the basement would flood a little after a heavy rain; we'd have to rush over there and put all the equipment up on pallets. We weren't about to complain: it was rent-free. And nobody could hear us down there, so that was great. The main thing is that we had nothing, and *anything* is better than nothing.

Dave's dad was an eye doctor who really wanted to be an actor. So he bought a theater. Look, if that's your dream and you can afford it, why not, right? Dr. Roth had this kind of oddball streak: he gave Dave a poster that said "To Thine Own Self Be True" with a picture of two chickens staring at a turkey. That was his sense of humor. He was a fun guy to talk to because his whole concept of entertainment was so radically different from ours— much more Broadway. Dr. Roth even wanted to help manage the band at one point. We had to say a more polite version of "no fucking way."

Dave's parents were divorced, which was unusual for that time. But his mom, Sibyl, was just as theatrical as his dad. Apparently, she told Dave that being a singer was a bad idea, and that if he was going to do it, he'd better be sure to have really good lighting. HA! She was a funny lady. When we first decided to start looking like a rock band, God bless her, Mrs. Roth would take us to stores and hold things up to us on hangers, saying, "Would you wear this? Would you wear that?" She was a lot of fun and really flamboyant. That's where Dave gets it.

He grew up with the show-tune-loving parents, and then there was his dad's brother, Uncle Manny, who gave Dave his first radio—Uncle Manny was a big influence. He'd opened a famous spot in Greenwich Village called Café Wha? in the early sixties when coffeehouses were the place to be. ("Manny coined the name by walking from couch to couch one night, saying, 'What shall we name our new coffeehouse?' And somebody would say, 'How 'bout "the Ever-Arcing Spiral of Transcendence"?' And Manny would go, 'Wha?' like Grandma would," according to Dave. "So eventually he named it Café Wha?") Lenny Bruce performed there, Bob Dylan, Joan Rivers, Allen Ginsberg, you name it. On his visits to New York City, Dave hung around and soaked in all the eccentricity and variety of that scene.

"I saw every kind of person and character and sex type in the Village at a very early age. I saw lesbians and knew what they were about, I saw the transvestite bunch and knew what they were about. I saw the Bensonhurst jock crowd, I saw uptown socialites, I saw debutantes come through the Café Wha? I saw royalty, and I saw junkies," he wrote. "I developed an appreciation—not just a tolerance, but an appreciation—for all types of people." Personally, I'd never be arrogant enough to assume I know what any group is *about* just because I encountered them in a bar. But that second part we had in common: Ed and I had already lived in two different countries, spoke two different languages, had seen enough of the world to know that people pretty much want the same things wherever you go. They want to feel good, and we knew it was our job to bring them that feeling when they came to see us play. Music is a viral way of spreading emotion.

The first song we played once Dave was in the band was "It's Your Thing" by the Isley Brothers, because that's what he wanted to do. It wasn't Zeppelin. It wasn't Deep Purple. It wasn't like any of the shit we grew up on. Clearly, Dave was from a different planet—a different musical *dimension*—than we were. "When I first joined the band, tried to sing some of the songs, there was Grand Funk Railroad, as well as Black Sabbath. The music was pretty alien to me. I didn't even own those records," Dave admits. "Did my best, which was awful, at the time, and the Van Halens were shocked and horrified."

True enough. But we saw being adaptable as part of being professional: *we can play anything*. So, we played "It's Your Thing." We never got any gigs when we auditioned with that song, though. So then you start tweaking things, you adjust. I forget who said it (probably my dad): if you play a song for the audience and they don't dance, don't play it again! Simple.

Look, I thought Dave was an odd duck. But what I respected was that he was willing to do the work, the same way we were. He understood it's audition, play, practice, audition, play, practice. Go, go, go, twenty-five hours a day. I don't think people grasp that to make it as a band, you have to work your ass to the bone: it's not *just* about partying and getting girls. (It was not lost on me, however, that Ringo got all the girls, and that he was a drummer with a big nose. Check. Check. If he could do it, I could do it.)

The first time we ever recorded together was in Dave's father's bedroom—I remember the greenish seventies carpet. We took apart the beds to use them as baffles. For first-time engineers, we actually weren't too bad. We'd seen pictures of recording studios; we got the general idea. You listen to the tape and if you have echo all over the place, you want to deaden it. It's not rocket science. I think the first song we recorded was called "Glitter." (Don't forget: Dave was obsessed with Ziggy Stardust and platforms and all that.) It wasn't terrible. But it wasn't really the direction I wanted to go in.

I remember being really unhappy with the sound. Now, you're working with cheesy material, lousy microphones, a bedroom that's not meant to be used as a studio, so, you know, good luck.

But in our minds, we're competing with guys like Jimmy Page. Even though we were younger—underage, at that point—you look up to the guys you grew up listening to, and it just didn't sound the same, and that killed us. We didn't understand that Jimmy Page was a seasoned studio professional who knew all the tricks to get drums mic'd the way they should be.

We had more trouble with our name. A cease-and-desist letter showed up from another band called Mammoth. Ed and I thought we should change our name to Rat Salad. (It's the title of a Black Sabbath song from the album *Paranoid*. But that's no excuse.) It was Dave's idea to change our name to Van Halen. "To anyone who knows him and his outsize ego this would seem to be an uncharacteristically magnanimous suggestion," our future manager Noel Monk has written about Dave's proposed name change, "but I don't think so. When it came to career aspirations David was nothing if not pragmatic. He wanted nothing less than to be famous and knew exactly what it would take to get him there." Dave studied *The Art of War*, and he knew: If you give somebody something, they're going to reciprocate. That'll make it easier for you to do what *you* want to do. From the very beginning, Dave knew he needed this band to get where he wanted to go. He's no fool: "Let's call ourselves Van Halen!"

I pretended not to like the idea, but we all knew it was right. Those three syllables are just fun to say—they feel good coming out of your mouth. "It sounds strong. It sounds like it has power to it," Dave said. "At the same time a classical piano player could be a Van Halen. Also in that way the band can evolve. If you call yourself the Electric Plotz, three years from now you're expected to sound like an Electric Plotz."

There was no such thing as "hard rock" or "heavy metal" at that point, but whatever sound we were going for, Van Halen was its name. And, obviously, it didn't hurt that it also happened to be *my* name, and Ed's.

More than anything, Van Halen was my dad's name. And though I never would have said this at the time, when I think about it now, it was in many ways my dad's band. Ed was asked by a journalist once what inspired him to play music. "My dad," he replied. "He was a soulful guy."

All the lessons our father taught us about music, energy, showmanship, and professionalism are what would eventually turn this bunch of teenagers in a basement in Pasadena into the biggest band in the world.

THE FOUR YEARS BETWEEN FOURTEEN and eighteen are a period of expansion and growth that's more intense than the next twenty years put together. You go through a lot of changes and you try to figure out, what is it you want? What are you going to do? How? And how do you find the right people who want to be on the ride together?

Most people don't. They don't put the time in. Or their parents don't think that they can do it. That's how we lost our first bass player, Mark Stone. Well, our first *real* bass player. Before him there was Mike Paloma. Then there was Frank—whose girlfriend got pregnant, and that was it for him. He hired us to play his wedding with his replacement, Kevin. Kevin was Black, and they tried to turn us away at the door of the wedding venue. I pulled out the contract and told them either they let us play the gig or I would sue them. They let us play. Kevin was a monster bass player, but unfortunately, he was also a monster pot smoker. Eventually he was replaced by Dennis. All this happened before I was sixteen, at which point we met Mark Stone.

We thought he was great, and apparently the feeling was mutual. "I knew it early on that they were both virtuosos," Mark said in a documentary about Van Halen that came out in 2003. "There were few legendary guitar players and I knew Edward was on his way to being there," he continued. "Alex was the leader. He was like the driving force that gave the band direction." Mark designed the very first Van Halen logo—the one where the V and the A's end in little balls, almost like music notes. He was a really nice, laid-back guy. But Ed and Dave and I had a different attitude about our careers: we were all in. Mark was torn. "I was a straight-A student in school, and doing the band, and I was split between these two things," Mark said in that doc, "and basically I just couldn't keep up with them."

I went and saw his widow after he died—just ten days after Ed, if you can believe that. (See you on the other side, Mark. We'll jam.) They lived in the house where Mark grew up. He'd bought it from his parents and he lived there forever. She told me that Mark's whole life, he felt like he missed his golden opportunity.

FIVE

We had a list of fourteen high schools and junior high schools within driving distance. . . . In every outside locker we'd put a flyer in. We'd flyer the place. If you saw Aerosmith was playing the football stadium, great, that's perfect, we'll flyer them. You could get, I believe, four thousand flyers for forty bucks at the instant press and we would break into teams. Ultimately, we had little walkie-talkies because the police would stop one team from flyering cars, and you would know that that was happening so you'd go into overdrive on the other side of the stadium so you could flyer every car. This built up a tremendous following for Van Halen on a very, very grassroots level. On the flyers we'd write, "The People's Choice." I got it from Muhammad Ali fight posters.

—*David Lee Roth*

Starting then, and for a long time to come, Dave and Ed and I were together *constantly*. We drove to the gigs together. We played the gigs together. We rehearsed together. We ate together. God knows we drank together. We spent countless hours in the middle of the night scouring Pasadena and the surrounding area for flood-lights we could steal from the outside of apartment complexes—then we'd use them for our shows. To say we were close kind of misses the point: we were one.

I couldn't smoke pot with Dave the way Ed could—that was their shared interest—because if I got stoned, I couldn't play, just could not do it. (Believe me, if marijuana had been conducive to my creativity or in any way beneficial to me as a drummer, I would have been a regular Rastafarian.) But Dave and I had mar-tial arts in common. When I was in high school, I took lessons from this guy Henry at International Karate on Colorado Boule-vard. Some of the other guys in my class were these real Paul Bunyan types, and I'd come out of there with welts on my arms from their karate chops. Well, that's not going to help with my drumming. I stopped when Henry put another student through a wall—the kid ended up with a collapsed sternum. More recently, I've trained with this guy who's like my Sicilian spiritual adviser. He keeps me disciplined, keeps the body ticking along after seventy years of use and abuse.

Back in the day, Dave and I would go to karate matches together at the Olympic Auditorium—it's fun to roll around with the roughhouse crowd, and that's who'd show up. Dave would give these crazy, incredible running commentaries on everything that was happening and the history of the moves going back to the shogun era. He had no idea what he was talking about half the time, but it didn't matter. He was fun to listen to. Very colorful. His brain was so weird that it was just interesting to be around.

Dave had an incredible work ethic. His dad was loaded and he was still shoveling shit at a horse stable to save up for a stereo! He didn't behave like a rich kid, maybe because he was so ambitious or maybe because he had so much to prove. For Ed and me, as foreigners without the benefit of much money, we were used to working our asses off and constantly coming up with work-arounds to compensate for the missing resources. One of the reasons Ed was always playing a Frankenstein guitar that he'd hammered together is that we were used to *everything* being like that. That's all we ever had: secondhand shit that we made the best of. "The main reason why I squeeze so many . . . call them tricks, call them techniques, out of the guitar was out of necessity because I couldn't afford the pedals," Ed said at the Smithsonian. "I couldn't afford a fuzz box and all the toys that everybody else had, so I did everything I could to get the sounds out of the guitar with my fingers."

We were forced to be improvisational. But everything was always falling apart. This is an old story but a true one: Ed drove a beat-up old Volvo, and to keep the door from falling off we strung it to the car with piano wire. It was literally hanging by a thread.

Along those same lines, our PA system blew up one night in 1974 when we had a gig at the Pasadena High School auditorium. Michael Anthony Sobolewski, the lead singer from the opening act, a band called Snake, was kind enough to offer us his. "I remember standing on the side of the stage watching Edward and Alex play and thinking, *Wow, these guys are good,*" he said. "Then Dave came up the side of the stage—I forget what he was dressed in, some kind of tux vest, but that was it, with a cane and a hat. He had long hair; I don't know if he had it colored, but I know he'd done something weird to it. And he said, 'How do you like my boys?'"

That led to us saying, "Hey, man, we should jam"—though I remember disliking aspects of Snake's performance. When they played the ZZ Top song "La Grange," Mikey would have his girl-friend run up onstage and pinch his nose so he sounded more like Billy Gibbons when he sang the "How, how, how, how"s. (Onstage!? That's sacred space. Ed and I were both aghast.) He came by the basement with his little brother, and that's where we learned that Michael Anthony Sobolewski wasn't just a nice guy, he could really sing—which was a good thing because back in the very beginning, we thought his sound on the bass was thin.

Mikey had passion and commitment. And he could do this thing with light pedals he rigged up to play with his feet, so we thought that was pretty cool. Though we didn't know it then, his falsetto enabled something that became important to the Van Halen sound: harmonies. The way his voice mixed with Ed's produced this really good sound that most Van Halen listeners mistake as just Mike's voice—their voices had this way of locking together.

I barely wanted to sing, let alone harmonize: I was busy bang-ing on drums. But once we had that particular mix of voices, it just started happening. Especially when we had to do all kinds of Top 40 covers in the clubs—that's what people wanted to get up and dance to, so it just naturally evolved. We all got better and better at it. We emulated bands like Humble Pie; they had tremendous, powerful vocals and they treated them like another instrument. The Beatles obviously did that, too. And once you had Queen, it kind of gave everyone permission—you could be a serious hard rock band and still have these beautiful harmonies laced throughout your songs.

So now we had Mikey, who lived right in the next town over, Arcadia. We were a party of four, just like Led Zeppelin. The original Van Halen lineup was ready to take on the world.

An interviewer asked my brother in the eighties, at the height of our success, when he knew that Van Halen was going to be something special. "I *always* thought Van Halen was going to be something special. To me, Van Halen was special when we played backyard parties," Ed replied. "Van Halen was always something special for me because it was *the main part of my life*."

TO CONVINCE OUR MOTHER WE were doing something legit, Ed and I both started taking music classes at Pasadena City College, where Mikey and Dave were studying, too. I thought we should sharpen our arrangement skills and be able to notate and all the rest of the stuff that comes with being a professional musician; I wanted us to have our bases covered. We studied with this guy Truman Fisher, whose other student of note was Frank Zappa. (Zappa would later thank Ed for "reinventing the electric guitar," so I'll always have a soft spot for the guy: see you on the other side, Frank.) "Dr. Fisher was very avant-garde and the one thing he taught me was fuck the rules," my brother said. "If it sounds good, it is good."

We figured out quickly, it's not what he's teaching you, it's how you interpret it, what you do with it. Ed and I wrote a couple arrangements for that class, and in my opinion, the first one was excellent. When you fly by the seat of your pants, interesting stuff can happen sometimes. The way Dave remembers it, "Alex Van Halen was knocking out eighteen-piece rock jazz ensemble arrangements for *West Side Story* that nobody could play, in 11/14 time—eleven beats per bar, and had to go from instrument to instrument, showing these befuddled students how to get to the first coda." Did I? Maybe something like that. (But there's no such thing as a fourteenth note, so there's no such thing as 11/14 time, Dave!!)

Dave never really got that into school; I don't think he could stand sitting still for that long. He's said he was "treading water until the band got launched," explaining, "I spent most of the time in junior college in music courses—theory and orchestration. I was not very good at it. Mathematically, I count to four and then start over . . . the Van Halens were far superior to anything I could do in that area—so was Michael. They won all the awards."

Another place Ed and I learned a lot during that time was sitting in front of the tube. The *Tonight Show* band was incredible. I love big band arrangements, and Doc Severinsen was great, how he put all that together, and of course there were Tommy Newsom and Ed Shaughnessy. And they did it every night! What better class can you have?

There were plenty of talented musicians at that junior college—guys who could play like nothing you've ever heard before. But what are you going to *do* with it? That's the question. How are you going to make a living?

You can't just sit in your closet all day making music for an audience of one. The only way you're going to make it in the music business is if your attitude is, *There's only one seat and who's going to take it? I'm taking it, motherfucker.*

When we used to play clubs, we learned just enough Top 40 songs to get hired. But you had to play forty-five-minute sets.

Even if you knew thirty songs, that was only enough to get you through two sets, because most Top 40 songs are only three minutes long. We figured we could play our own stuff, and no one would care as long as the beat was there. One day we were playing at this club in Covina called Posh—I'll never forget this. We ran out of Top 40 tunes, so we started playing our own music. The owner of the club walks up to us while we were playing a song and goes, "Stop! I hired you to play Top 40. What is this shit?" It was always that way. It was either "the guitarist is too loud" or "plays too psychedelic." They always complained about me. It's funny, but no matter how hard I tried to sound like the records—and I really tried—I always ended up sounding like me.

—Edward Van Halen

So we didn't do our own songs; we did what everyone already wanted to hear.

But we tried to play it better than the next guy—whatever "better" means. More articulately, in a more limber, interpretive way. And we had high standards for stagecraft; we'd learned that from my dad. Just a lot of little things, like you never leave the audience hanging: you're always either playing or chatting them up, you never turn your back to them. You can't stop in the middle of the set and start tuning your instrument—that's not only disrespectful, you're changing the flow of everything. You've got half an hour. Let's make that half hour count!

We tried to create a spectacle. Obviously, there was Dave, with all his vibrating energy, yakking away and jumping around in skin-tight pants. Then there was "the Bomb": a big, heavy army surplus

World War II metal torpedo casing that my brother used as an effects rack. (He sawed open a hole in the side of the thing and stuffed in an echo box and tape delay.) It was taller than him and impressive to behold. Eventually I got a second bass drum, which added to the grandeur—my heroes used them, Ginger Baker, Keith Moon. And finally, we had the smoke pots.

We made them out of empty cat food tins bolted to a two-by-four and filled with 4F black gunpowder, the stuff used by people who make their own bullets. (You could only get two cans of the stuff at a time, so before a show, we'd all go separately to get our allotments. God knows why they thought four long-haired nineteen-year-olds were regularly stocking up on 4F.) Then we'd wire the thing up and connect it to a foot switch, and we'd detonate it when we started playing. It was madness. "I would scream, 'Ladies and gentlemen, please welcome the amazing Van Halen,' and we'd hit the first note and fire off half the smoke pots. It looked like Tiananmen Square," as Dave remembers it. "People would be running, gasping, crying from all the smoke. If it was an indoor dance and we'd miscalculated the ventilation, it was like playing in a cloud. . . . Regularly, something onstage would catch fire and have to be put out."

Dave had an Opel Kadett station wagon, and we would pile in there with our gear and play anywhere it would take us. Biker bars. Bowling alleys. Hispanic car clubs. Backyard parties that were always getting shut down by the cops; the biggest of them would be nearly a thousand people. Roller rinks. Local establishments with names like Perkins Palace, Barnacle Bill's, the Proud Bird. There was this place called the International Casino where the ceiling was so low that you would bang your head if you stood up too fast from the drum kit, and the "dressing room" was a urinal with a pipe that went into the ground but wasn't connected to anything. You had to get there early before it stank so bad it made your eyes tear.

It's okay. That's our job. Every band goes through that shit. If you want it bad enough, you just have to suck it up.

I remember one night at a place called Walter Mitty's in a lower-income area in Pomona, all of a sudden the whole place empties out while we're playing—someone had been knifed. We saw the poor guy with his stomach spilling out. We had to play there again the next night, and in our infinite wisdom, we placed the amps a few feet away from the wall so that if the shit hit the fan again, we could jump behind them for protection.

When you get to a ratty club and the audience starts to drink and the music is thundering and people are moving around, it's always a milder version of Altamont. The pattern is: people get drunk, they start pushing each other, a fight breaks out. Most of the time we managed to keep it under control because the last thing we needed was people brawling at our gig. We were there to unite, not divide.

We had a repertoire of about three hundred songs. We never had a rhythm guitarist, so Ed was pushed into a situation where anytime there was a dead spot he would fill it, and that became his style. But every club had its own playlist and we had to cater to that. If you're at a Latino place, you have to play whatever gets them up and dancing—you're not there to struggle with the audience, you're not there to convert them. You're there to kind of ease them into your sound, because ultimately people don't remember what you played. They remember how you made them feel.

The beauty of rock 'n' roll is that it appeals to everybody. And nobody goes to put on a show and thinks, *I hope nobody shows up.*

You're there because you're proud of what you have put together and you want to share it with as many people as possible. Our dad always told us: don't take sides on anything or you've just cut your audience in half. That's why we were permanently and resolutely apolitical.

There was a club called the Gas Company and there was a band that played there all the time called Gold. They were very, very good. This was upstairs, behind the pool hall in Pasadena. Ed and I would go there whenever we didn't have a gig to listen to those guys and obsess: What were they playing that was making it work? Why are they here and we're stuck at the place with the busted urinal?

We were so hungry to succeed that we gave it everything we had every single time we performed. I remember thinking, *I hope we don't have to do this all night, every night, after we get signed.* (Little did I know.) That's why Cream only lasted three years— they couldn't keep it going like that. It's physically and creatively unnatural to play at that level every night. Even if you're Ginger Baker.

You have to remember, at that time, drum solos were the shit. That was like the highlight of the evening. It kind of got old, and people don't want to hear drum solos anymore now. But at the time the pressure was on. One of the scariest things my dad ever said to me was, "When the drums come in, the song goes to the next level."

Here's what we knew for sure, from the very beginning. We're not there to perform a song. We're there to provide the energy to celebrate. We weren't being recorded; you had to be there, in the flesh, to have the experience with us. We're there to instigate something with the audience. Van Halen is there to make the party.

Did we take it too far sometimes? Well, yeah. One night we were playing the Golden West Ballroom in Norwalk, California—great facility; it had a good stage and some lighting, capacity of about a thousand. Ed snorts some coke after the gig. So far it's a regular Friday night. But it turns out not to be coke: he's just vacuumed up some monster lines of PCP or who knows what, maybe horse tranquilizer. Somebody came running up to me and said, "Man, you better go check out your brother, he's not looking so good."

Bit of an understatement. I took one look at Ed—his blank eyes, his green skin, his mouth drooping open—and said, "Get him to the emergency room. NOW." I remember literally falling to my knees and praying (or more like begging, who am I kidding?), *Please don't let him die.* But he did! They literally pronounced him dead upon arrival when the ambulance pulled up at the hospital.

Fortunately, human beings make mistakes, even doctors. Ed came back around after a few seconds.

It would not be the last time I was afraid I was going to lose him, unfortunately, or the last time it came damn close to happening.

SIX

No, I don't ask for permission
This is my chance to fly
Maybe enough ain't enough for you
But it's my turn at a try.

—*Van Halen, "Unchained"*

We knew we couldn't spend the rest of our lives playing Pasadena. And only nineteen miles—but a *universe*—away was the Sunset Strip. Starting in the spring of 1974, that became our hunting ground.

The hot spots were the Whisky a Go Go (and yes, that's how they spell it) and the Roxy, where we couldn't even get auditions. The club scene was very segregated—if you didn't have a record deal, you couldn't play here, you could only play there, that kind of thing. Or there were places like the Troubadour, where you couldn't really be rock 'n' roll, you had to be a singer-songwriter type of act, or something softer like the Eagles.

And then there was Gazzarri's. It was kind of down and dirty and had a seedy vibe to it. "Bill Gazzarri hired whoever he could get for the cheapest," as Mikey put it. The Doors played there regularly before they got signed; that was Gazzarri's claim to fame. But the crowd was mostly tourists—definitely not a Hollywood clientele.

Didn't matter. It was our way into the legend of the Sunset Strip, our point of access.

We auditioned once or twice for Bill Gazzarri, the owner, and he was not impressed—just stared at us, in our T-shirts and jeans, chewing on his cigar and shaking his head. Dave still thought Ed and I were aesthetically underwhelming: "He always told me I looked like shit," Ed said, "so around the time we auditioned for Gazzarri's on the Sunset Strip, I got some platforms and nearly broke my ankles."

Look, we were willing to try anything to get noticed. But ultimately we made it to Gazzarri's on what we did best. Some bookers Mr. Gazzarri worked with saw us play at Pasadena City College. By that time, if we played anywhere in the area at least a thousand people would show up, and we must have been smoking that night, because the bookers were really impressed. They convinced Mr. Gazzarri to give us a few nights to show him what we could do with a crowd.

It did not go well. Ed had bought a battered Econoline van, and we drove in around noon to have our sound check the day of our first gig. But there's only so much you can do in an empty venue; you have to adjust everything once the crowd is actually there. So that's done, it's one thirty, now what? I'd heard John Bonham, the drummer for Zeppelin, say that even if you're nervous before a gig, you don't dare start drinking, because then you'll be tired—or worse—by the time you're onstage. So drinking was out. We spent the rest of the day sitting in the van, getting antsier and more anxious by the minute. God knows why; I guess we felt like we had to be close to our equipment.

We're talking about 1974. America had just gotten out of Vietnam and Watergate. There was a lot of crime and a big recession, and you could feel it in all kinds of ways. We saw it every time we looked at the Hollywood sign—which was supposed to be this iconic symbol of glamour but instead was crumbling to pieces. (It got worse and worse until 1978, when a bunch of people decided to raise money and save the thing. Alice Cooper—who was always around at the clubs on the Strip in the seventies—donated $28,000 to save the letter O.)

To Mr. Gazzarri's horror, probably four people showed up that first night we performed—*nobody* was there. Well, that ain't gonna fly. Club owners make their money selling booze, so we learned fast: you got to get them dancing, because the more they dance, the more they drink. Four people having a blast can outdance and outdrink fourteen people who are just sitting around acting like they're in a library.

We would glue four or five songs together and Dave would banter in between to keep people up on their feet, engaged with us. Working the crowd in a club is like trying to catch a fish: pull too hard, come on too strong, be *too* obnoxious, and you'll lose the fish. But if you're timid, you're never going to reel them in, either. You need confidence. Courage!

Mr. Gazzarri liked to think of himself as the "Godfather of Rock 'n' Roll," and he did what he could to make his place a party; he hired house dancers to shimmy around in little outfits. ("My sister was a Gazzarri's dancer for a very brief period of time, and her picture was on the wall there," Michael said. "I remember flipping out when we started playing there, going, 'You got to be kidding me.'") There was something fun and loose about how unfashionable and unprofessional Gazzarri's was. I mean, there were wet T-shirt contests. (Which I had a big problem with. HA!)

When it was hopping, Gazzarri's was a good time: just a lot of middle-class people partying, and that was their Hollywood experience. At the end of that first weekend, Mr. Gazzarri handed us seventy-five bucks to split four ways, which was barely enough to cover our gas and beer. But he told us to keep coming back.

THE WHOLE DAY WAS GEARED toward the night. The day was nothing. Night was when we came to life.

We played three sets a night, almost every night. It was grueling; only really young people can function that way. And it's not like the night was over when we finished performing at one or two in the morning—it was just getting started. We were a bunch of dudes on the loose in Hollywood, unsupervised! And all around us were some of the greatest music clubs in the world. The Strip was a rock 'n' roll playground.

We were aware of being literally in the midst of our idols. John Lennon got kicked out of the bar above the Roxy, just down the block from Gazzarri's, for partying too hard around the same time we started playing there. "You guys, you won't believe who I just saw: *Keith Richards and Ringo Starr*," Dave told us one night after he'd been gluing up our posters and passing out flyers in front of the Roxy. Gazzarri's was next to the Rainbow Bar & Grill, and between sets one night we saw John Bonham there, drinking with Ritchie Blackmore, the guitarist from Deep Purple. Ed and I were freaking out: *Deep Purple and Zeppelin at one table?* We thought our heads would explode. We went over to introduce ourselves and invite them to hear us play next door. Bonham took one look at us and said, "Who *are* you? Fuck off." He was hammered, and when I went to shake his hand, he took a swing at me. His bodyguard stopped him from actually hitting me, but I almost wish he hadn't. It would have been an honor to get popped by Bonham! That's what we thought of them.

The most important thing was that we were all getting better at what we were doing, both musically and as entertainers. The line between the stage and the audience? We made that disappear. We learned how to connect with a big group of people on an emotional level—how to draw them in and make them feel like they were part of what we were doing. Indispensable.

You develop timing and phrasing within the band when you play over and over (and over) again with the same people. You can't get that any other way than putting in the hours. It's like having a dance partner: you get used to each other. Ed would always tune his guitar a quarter step down—to somewhere between E and D sharp—to accommodate Dave's limited range, make his voice sound its best. When you work together like that to highlight everyone's strengths, you end up becoming greater than the sum of your parts. Which is really saying something when one of the parts is a virtuoso like my brother.

We learned a lot. We figured out that if somebody throws a bottle, or an amp blows up, or a fight breaks out, first thing you do, play James Brown. Get them clapping, take their minds off it. (You need horns to do a James Brown song any justice, but we didn't have any. Instead, we did what we'd always done and came up with a work-around. We made the vocals into our horn section—which had the desirable side effect of forcing us to get better at harmonies.) Humor always saves the day, and Dave was very funny and self-effacing. (Then, anyway.) Van Halen got very, very good at getting people fired up, dancing, amped. That was our gift as a group.

If you don't know where the term "rock 'n' roll" comes from, look it up. You're there to get people in the mood, to free them of their inhibitions. Once word gets around that there's a band that's good at that—and they're playing five, six nights a week—people start to show up. More dancing bodies means more drinking means more money. So, Mr. Gazzarri was getting happier and happier with us. "The girls would always say to me, 'Godfather, could you introduce me to Eddie?' Eddie was the quiet one, but he was the most popular," Gazzarri once told a journalist. "He would be on the side of the stage, and every week that we played them here, there would be at least fifty girls who would come and pay and sit on Eddie's side all night long."

I know: sounds like fun.

And it was. But even though my mom kept on yelling at us to get a job and wear a suit, we were already professionals, to be perfectly honest. We took our work very seriously. And we kept getting raises as more and more people came to see us. We thought of the Beatles and their residency at the Star-Club in Hamburg, Germany, and we felt good about doing our own version of that in Hollywood. Plus there were a *lot* of women. "Gazzarri's, they'd have like a *Playboy* night and it was, 'Holy shit!' Girls were every-where," the drummer Mick Brown says in *Nöthin' but a Good Time*, a book about the hard rock scene on the Strip. "When I went there I thought I was in the movies."

So life was good. For a while.

You kind of knew if you could get two hundred people to get up and go crazy, you could do it with twenty thousand. I'm not saying that out of arrogance, it's just something we could sense. Not to mention the fact that Ed was a phenomenal player who was only getting better and better. Among other things, he was perfecting his tapping—it's when a guitarist sounds the notes by using both his picking hand and his fretting hand to tap the fretboard, or in Ed's case, *hammer* it. "Tapping is like having a sixth finger on your left hand," is how he explained it. "Instead of picking, you're hitting a note on the fretboard. I was just sitting in my room at home, drinking a beer, and I remembered seeing other players using the technique for one quick note in a solo. I thought, 'Well, nobody is really capitalizing on that idea.' So I started dicking around and realized the potential."

Ed never claimed he invented tapping. Paganini did it on violin in the 1600s! Steve Hackett, the guitarist of (the other) Genesis, tapped on the *Nursery Cryme* album in 1971. Harvey Mandel did some two-handed tapping on his album *Shangrenade* in 1973. A guy named Emmett Chapman even invented a whole ten-stringed electric tapping instrument—the "Chapman Stick"—in 1974. But Ed became the uncontested master of the technique; he made it his own in a way that blew people's minds. It was so different from anything anyone else was doing that Dave told Ed he should turn his back to the audience at Gazzarri's when he was tapping so they wouldn't know what he was doing or how. "There were a lot of guitar players that started trying to copy Eddie's tapping and all the hammer-on stuff that he was doing," Michael recalled. "A lot of gigs that we would play, Dave would say, 'Hey, we don't want all these guitar players stealing your stuff.'" We told Dave to go fuck himself. You *never* turn your back on the audience. That's showmanship 101. If you ever see Ed turn away, it's just because he's manipulating distortion sounds by facing his amps.

With some of our Gazzarri's money we rented session time at Cherokee Studios in Chatsworth. There are some tracks from that 1974 recording that don't really sound like Van Halen—Dave crooning and whispering and so on. But we also did early versions of "Take Your Whiskey Home" and "In a Simple Rhyme," which both ended up on our third album and, if you ask me, are classic Van Halen songs. We were already making original music that was true to our ultimate vision as a band.

The only problem was that we couldn't do our songs at Gazzarri's. We had to keep churning out covers of whatever was on the radio. (Not that it was all bad. We played the Kinks *into the ground*.) We weren't really treated like musicians there, more like a four-headed human jukebox. "We were supposed to get people into the bar, not into the band," as my brother put it.

Look, it could have been a hell of a lot worse: my old man had to play German propaganda songs at gunpoint! Compared to that, pounding out "You Really Got Me" four million times is paradise, obviously. All we had to do was play music for money while people partied. It's not like we were cleaning toilets (again: something my father did when we got to this country, without ever complaining, to make ends meet). We knew that we were lucky.

Bill Gazzarri was a good guy and I'll always be grateful to him, but it's bullshit when he says he discovered us. He didn't even know our names. He actually thought Dave was called "Van" Halen, like Van Morrison.

Weeks turned into months. Months turned into several years. And do you remember how long a year was when you were young? I was in my early twenties, but I felt like life was passing me by. At the end of the day, we were still just the house band at a bar, and that wasn't going to cut it. I didn't want to be fifty years old, smoking cigarettes in line down at the Local 47, wearing some shiny-ass pair of pants. And there was no way I was going to let that happen to a brilliant musician like Ed.

Music industry people were not coming to Gazzarri's. We knew we needed to get onstage somewhere we could get more exposure, get signed. Mr. Gazzarri told us: you play anywhere else, you're not welcome here anymore.

Eventually we had to tell him, "That's okay with us, Mr. Gazzarri. Thanks for everything."

BEFORE HE WAS THE "PRINCE OF POP," the DJ with the best-known show in radio for twenty years, Rodney Bingenheimer was the "Mayor of the Sunset Strip." They made a documentary about him by that name, and everyone is in it kissing his ass: Mick Jagger, Alice Cooper, David Bowie, Debbie Harry, Neil Young. The guy was connected. He came to town in the midsixties and pretty soon he was living with Sonny and Cher, doing their publicity. For a while he had his own club on the Strip called the English Disco; maybe you've heard of it. It was shut down before we showed up, but he was still everywhere—this short little guy with a quiet voice and a mop of bangs, like a West Coast Andy Warhol. He looked so much like Davy Jones that when Rodney auditioned for the Monkees and he didn't get the gig, they still kept him around as a body double for Jones on their movies.

Anyway, one night in 1976, Rodney saw us play at Gazzarri's, and he knew what he was seeing. "The crowd was just incredible. A lot of girls; I always thought that bands that had a lot of girls going crazy were gonna make it big," he said. We told Rodney he should drop by and see our show at the Pasadena Civic Auditorium and hear some of our original material. "When I got there, they had something like two thousand kids in the place," Rodney told the *Los Angeles Times* a year later. "They had put the show together themselves. Amazing." It was a production getting those shows together; he's right. You had to pay for the lights and pay for the security, you had to kind of patch it all together—the whole thing could feel a bit like being an imitation of a *real* band, because you're coming up with all these weird, half-assed, Band-Aid solutions to problems you don't totally understand because you're not a promoter or a designer or an engineer, you're a MUSICIAN!

Because Rodney talked us up, we started getting booked at the Starwood on Santa Monica Boulevard. "I spoke to this guy Ray who was at the Starwood at the time and he said, 'Well I don't know. We've never heard of Van Halen and they're a Gazzarri's band,'" Rodney says in *Nöthin' but a Good Time*. "Back then, if a band was labeled a Gazzarri's band, they never played outside of Gazzarri's. But I said, 'Yeah, these guys attract a lot of beer drinkers,' and he said maybe they'd give it a shot." It became one of our favorite spots.

You could play in front of a thousand people at the Starwood! And they had full light, full sound, and a much bigger stage than over at the Whisky, where we also started performing after we finished our Gazzarri's run. I loved the Whisky a Go Go; I think it was probably the best place of all for us. For one thing, it was the birthplace of go-go dancers in cages! But what the Whisky *really* had on the Starwood—on all the clubs—was this amazing backstage area covered in graffiti written by the giants of rock 'n' roll: poems by Jim Morrison scrawled on the ceiling; signatures from Janis Joplin, Jimi Hendrix, Led Zeppelin, you name it. It made you feel like you were part of something bigger than just your own band, being there, like you were a part of what Leonard Cohen called the "Tower of Song."

One night, Rodney brought Gene Simmons from Kiss to the Starwood to check us out. We were good that night. We were opening for a band called the Boyz, and their guitar player George Lynch has said, "All I cared about was that they didn't suck and drive people away before our set. Then to see everything you thought you knew about guitar playing change right before your eyes at your very own show? Talk about depressed!" Ed had that effect on his fellow guitar players: they didn't know whether to be excited or suicidal when they discovered someone could play like my brother.

Gene knew he was seeing something special. "The guitar player—I didn't know their names or anything—he steps up and starts doing this stuff and tapping, which I'd never seen before," Gene recollected, after Ed passed, of that first time he saw us at the Starwood. "And he was playing not only fast and furious, but sometimes in harmony on the tapping. I just was so astonished. I was waiting backstage by the third song."

Gene rushed over to us as soon as we finished performing. "He's going, 'You guys got a record deal? You guys got a manager?'" my brother remembered. "We're going, 'No. What's a manager? What's a record deal?'" Gene had just started a company called Man of a Thousand Faces, and his plan was to extend his reach by finding new acts—Gene was always as much an entrepreneur as a performer. He was going to fly us to New York and put us up in a hotel so he could produce our demo, he said, all excited and talking a mile a minute. "But your name! Van Halen sounds like a shirt company," Gene insisted. That was his only criticism. He thought we should call ourselves Virus or Daddy Longlegs, and he had an idea for our new and improved logo. "I probably still have a copy of the drawing somewhere packed away," Michael said. "There was a picture of a spider, you could see the bottom half of the spider with the legs coming out, and then on his head he had a top hat or something. And we're like, 'Hmmmmm.' We weren't really going for it, but you know, he was in the business and we weren't."

We politely declined Gene's suggestions. But we were obviously thrilled that he wanted to produce our record. Gene was funny and generous, and it seemed like our dream was plowing toward reality. This was *it*.

We didn't know it at the time, but the other band playing that night thought it was going to be *their* big break: Gene had come intending to scope them. "Obviously Van Halen got picked to go to New York and record demos with Gene Simmons instead of us," their drummer, Mick Brown, said. "As soon as that door was opened, Van Halen went in and that was slammed shut." That's the thing about the music industry: it's a zero-sum game.

It was the first time Ed and I had been to New York City since we'd docked there after the boat ride from Holland as kids. I remember being baffled by the way the liquor stores didn't sell beer, or my go-to, Schlitz Malt Liquor—for that you had to go to delis, where they didn't sell liquor! Made no sense.

We had a great time with Gene—I remember he took us shopping for leather pants, which he insisted we couldn't possibly be without if we were serious about becoming rock stars. (I mean, look who you're asking: imagine Kiss without black leather. You can't.) The main event was recording at Electric Lady, the studio Jimi Hendrix had founded in 1968 right in the heart of Greenwich

Village. We tracked fifteen songs, including "Runnin' with the Devil," "On Fire," and "House of Pain." None of it sounded good, though: the recording sucked and our performance wasn't really up to snuff. "I learned that I didn't like overdubbing," Ed said of the experience. "Gene just naturally assumed that I knew that was how it's done, but I said, 'Oh no, I can't do that.' I wanted to stick to my normal way of playing, where I would noodle in between chord lines. Instead, I had to fill in those spots on the tape after I recorded the rhythm part, so it was rather uncomfortable."

Look, we were young, we were opinionated, we were full of piss and vinegar and all that. We were also delusional, because we were not as good as we thought we were. But we were better than everyone else thought.

Gene took us to meet Kiss's manager Bill Aucoin and play our demo for him. I'll never forget this: we get to his office and he puts his feet up on the desk and gets a shoe shine. It was so obnoxious we really couldn't believe it. He passed on us, but I like to think we would have passed on him given the chance. We were as un-impressed with him as he was with us, that's for sure.

Gene's a great man and I love him. I'll always appreciate his early enthusiasm for us and understanding of what we were doing. He's even been humble about it: "I was just honored and lucky enough to be there to witness the greatness before it exploded on the world," he said. "This whole idea of 'you discovered Van Halen,' the people who literally discovered the Van Halen brothers were their mom and dad. After that, the two brothers made themselves. Nobody handed them anything. They worked hard for it. They put the years in." Thanks, Gene. That we did.

When we got back home, Rodney Bingenheimer played some of our songs from the demo on his show *Rodney on the ROQ*; KROQ was the radio station in Pasadena. But we were still disappointed that more hadn't come of the whole thing. We'd thought that was going to be our big break and we were going to get signed and take over the world.

"The world's most expensive demo tape," my brother once called our Gene Simmons recording in *Guitar World*. "We didn't know where to take it. We didn't feel like walking around to people's doors saying 'Sign us, sign us.' We just kept playing everywhere and eventually they came to us."

WHAT WE DIDN'T KNOW AT the time was that there's a way in which the club days were the pinnacle of our experience on planet Earth. *That's* when we got the highest highs, because the potential of being great was still out there! That's when the dream of Van Halen was the most magical—because it was still a dream. There's nothing more exciting than thinking you're on the verge of achieving everything you've ever wanted. Including achieving it.

A journalist once asked Ed if there was anything he missed about our club days. This was decades later, long after we'd had multiple platinum records and toured the world and made real money. "I miss how things back then were unknown," Ed said. "There was no internet or YouTube, so we got away with a lot of things in certain aspects of life that bands would never get away with today. It was easier to build things up and get a reputation. I miss the mystique."

I miss the ambition. The sense of purpose. The yearning.

Oscar Wilde said it best: "The suspense is terrible. I hope it will last."

SEVEN

I put my heart and my soul into my work and have lost
my mind in the process.

—*Vincent van Gogh*

The thing about making music is that when you get to something really good, it doesn't feel like you've created it, it feels
more like you've *found* it—like that song or that lick has always
existed and was just waiting for you to play it. It's probably the
same way with painting and poetry and every other art form—
when you finally hit it, there's just something about the sound
or the look or whatever it is that feels meant to be. Think of the
chord progression in "Jump" . . . can you imagine that melody
not existing? It's almost inconceivable.

But it's torture along the way. You're groping in the dark. As
inevitable as a great song feels, that's how *un*sure and frustrated
you feel until you get there.

I read something an art critic named Jerry Saltz posted on
social media about this the other day that really summed it up.

"Artists: your work hides from you until you find it. The beauty is that it loves being found as much as you love finding it. You have touched the tail of the dragon." You're never going to get your arms around the whole thing . . . you'll probably spend your entire life wondering if dragons exist, even after you've touched one. As in: Is that sound even really out there? If we work hard enough, if we play long enough, will we eventually hear the sound of our dreams coming out of our instruments? Or will it always be just out of reach, just around the corner?

That's what drove us. That's what drives every artist, musician, writer, sculptor, you name it. People who have to be creative, who don't know any other way to exist, just keep grinding away at whatever their mode of expression is.

I shouldn't say grinding, because most of the time it was fun as hell for us. That's the amazing thing about music: you don't have to make it alone, you can make it with your brother and your buddies at clubs where people are drinking and dancing and pretty girls are smiling at you because you're in the band.

Sure, Ed spent more hours than anyone could ever count on the edge of his bed with his guitar, playing around, creating. But he spent even more time jamming with me, and whoever else happened to be around—Brian and Kevin, Mark Stone, Dave Roth, whoever.

Comradery was part of our job.

NINETEEN SEVENTY-SEVEN WAS OUR YEAR.

In January, we opened for Santana at Long Beach Arena . . . our biggest gig to date. Then we opened for Nils Lofgren at the Santa Monica Civic Auditorium. The *Los Angeles Times* called us "the slickest and most commercially promising band on the Hollywood scene." We headlined a string of packed shows at the Whisky. A guy named Marshall Berle had been doing the booking there, and he liked us. Marshall was Milton Berle's nephew, and he'd been an agent earlier in his career, so he knew a lot of people. He was the one who convinced Ted Templeman, an executive at Warner Bros., that he needed to see us perform.

On February 2, Ted showed up at the Starwood, not that we knew he was there. He looked like any other long-haired Malibu thirtysomething hippie, just blonder. But Ted was already a big deal; he'd worked with Van Morrison, the Doobie Brothers, Clapton, and Montrose. His arrival at the Starwood that night marked the beginning of the next phase of our lives.

To hear him tell it, Ted's interest in us was immediate. "When Van Halen came onstage, it was like they were shot out of a cannon. Their energy wowed me," Ted wrote in his book, *Ted Templeman: A Platinum Producer's Life in Music*. "They played like they were performing in an arena and not a small Hollywood club." Like I said, we had a gift for getting people up and moving, whether there were dozens of them or thousands. The night that Ted first came to see us, there were actually very few. Maybe seven people had materialized . . . and three of them were our girlfriends.

We'd just played Long Beach and we had a big gig coming up at the Pasadena Civic, so our home crowd wasn't exactly flooding the Starwood that night. Didn't matter. Ted could tell it was our musicianship that set us apart. He continued:

Their guitar player blew my mind. Right out of the gate, I was just knocked out by Ed Van Halen. It's weird to say this but encountering him was almost like falling head over heels in love with a girl on a first date. I was so dazzled. I had never been as impressed with a musician as I was with him that night. I'd seen Miles Davis, Dave Brubeck, Dizzy Gillespie, all of these transcendent artists, but Ed was one of the best musicians I'd ever seen live. His choice of notes, the way he approached his instrument, reminded me of saxophonist Charlie Parker. In fact, as I watched I was thinking there were two musicians in my mind who were the absolute best of the best: Parker, jazz pianist Art Tatum, and now here's the third game-changer, Ed Van Halen.

I don't agree with much of what Ted wrote in his book, but I'm definitely with him on that.

Things started happening—fast. It was like a cascade of dominos knocking each other over. Every obstacle to our dream becoming reality just cleared out of the way. Ted convinced his boss Mo Ostin, the CEO of Warner Bros., to come with him to the Starwood to see us for himself the next night. Mo loved us. "That was a heavy thing," my brother said. "I remember talking to other bands and they've always been trying to get Ted to produce their records . . . there he was. Within a week, we were signed. It was right out of the movies."

They told us they wanted us, and God knows we wanted them, but they couldn't deal with us unless we had a manager. Marshall Berle was there, and he was the one who'd recommended us to Ted: suddenly, he was our manager. The day after that gig we went into the Warner Bros. office in Burbank and signed a letter of intent.

Like I said: *fast.* It was a nice change of pace from how we'd been feeling, like it was taking forever for our real lives to start. Now we were in a state of euphoria. Our heads were swimming as we took in the new reality: *This is actually happening.* You could feel the momentum building and building, and Van Halen's ascent just started to seem . . . inevitable. There's no high like that. When you can feel the wind in your sails and life just seems to *want* you to have it all.

A few weeks later we drove back to Burbank in Dave's beat-up car to sign our contract and meet the people we'd be working with. We drove most of the way, that is. We ran the rest. Dave's car—a decrepit red Valiant, at that particular point—broke down a few miles before the exit off the Ventura Freeway. We were all wearing our platform shoes, which made sprinting to the Warner Bros. offices a real mission.

We made quite an impression. "They finally showed up looking not just disheveled, which is what I had expected, but utterly exhausted," Noel Monk, the guy Warner had tapped to be our road manager, said about that first meeting. (Noel's claim to fame was that he'd been the Sex Pistols' road manager, which tells you how the record label was seeing us, who they thought was a comparable act.) "I don't mean that they looked like they'd been up all night living up to their reputation," Noel continued. "Instead, they were red-faced and sweaty and breathing heavily. They looked like they had just competed in some kind of athletic event—and lost."

Maybe so. But we felt like we'd won. Even running that last five miles was almost fun because we felt like we were physically expressing our commitment to the band, the label, the process. Nothing was going to stop us now. It was finally happening—we were going to have a record.

The name Van Halen was going to mean something, not just to us, not just to a couple thousand kids in Southern California.

If we were as good as we thought, we were walking right into the future we'd dreamed of . . . joining our heroes.

MO OSTIN WAS A BADASS record executive. He started out as Frank Sinatra's accountant. He signed the Kinks and the Jimi Hendrix Experience to Reprise when he was working there. He had a real Picasso on the wall of his office at Warner Bros.! Ed and I were in absolute awe of him. I can't exactly blame the guy for being good at his job, but maybe he did it a little too well: he gave us a terrible contract.

Later, we were told it was a "Motown contract," or, to put it in much uglier terms, someone else said we'd signed an N-word contract. Whatever you call it, it all amounts to the same thing: young musicians with talent but no leverage will do anything to get signed by a major label. That's all we wanted on earth. And they knew that. They knew that we'd take what we were given and not ask too many questions about the terms—even though we'd heard all the horror stories from the acts who'd come before us. I read *Star-Making Machinery: Inside the Business of Rock and Roll*, which was a bestseller at the time, and I gave it to Dave to read, too. We knew we were getting a crummy deal and that there wasn't a lot we could do about it. (Of course, it's all relative. "Van Halen got signed first. They got a great deal," Kelly Garni, the original bassist for Quiet Riot, has complained. "*We* got the shitty deal.")

In a perfect world, our manager, Marshall, would have been thinking ahead, looking out for our interests, and getting us more favorable terms. But that didn't happen; the whole deal came together so quickly that night at the Starwood. Ted remembers:

"During our backstage visit, Mo pulled Marshall and me aside. Mo said to Marshall, 'Do they have a manager?' 'No, I'm just kind of looking after them.' 'Well, they do now. You're their manager.' Right there, we made the deal. I was ecstatic." (I'll bet you were, Ted! You can't do better than negotiating against someone who owes you their job.)

It's hard to know how to feel: Should I be grateful to Marshall for getting Ted to come and see us, and grateful to Ted for getting Mo to sign us? (I am! Thanks, guys. You're the best. We love you.) Or should I resent the industry for making money off our sweat and talent without paying us what we're worth? (I do! Greedy motherfuckers!) But I'm getting ahead of myself. All we knew that day was that we were the real deal, a band with a recording contract.

And you know what? If I had the choice, I doubt I'd do *any* of it differently, even with the benefit of hindsight.

Ted would produce our first album. We had already been working on our songs for years, so we had a lot to choose from when we got into the studio to make our demo for Warner Bros. "A lot of the basic ideas were things that I came up with when I used to practice on the edge of my bed," Ed said of those songs. "Sometimes you have to work for inspiration. But ultimately, it's not really work because my brother and I genuinely love to jam. I'd say that's the way most things happen in our band. It usually begins with me and Al, which is funny in a way, because most people don't usually think of the guitar and drums as a unit . . . I think Al's drumming is more musical because he listens to me rather than just being concerned with maintaining a steady groove."

Ed and I were locked in. We'd literally spent our lives getting unified in that way, playing the same thing over and over again, waiting for the next chord to reveal itself. I needed to hear what he was doing and he needed to hear what I was doing, and together we got the job done. "All I had in my monitors when we played live was Al's drums," Ed has said. "A little bit of Dave's vocals, a little bit of mine, a little bit of Mike's vocals. But all I hear is myself and my brother."

EIGHT

Ted took us to Sunset Sound in the spring of 1977, with Donn Landee, his favorite engineer—who would ultimately become ours, too, and one of Ed's closest collaborators. But that took time. Early on we disagreed with Donn about all kinds of things.

Within fifteen minutes of starting the session, Donn said, "Take the front drumheads off." Well, the drum makes its sound from the resonance *of* the drumheads—you don't want just one or it sounds very flat. But that's the sound that was in fashion at the time. The guys who *I* liked—Bonham, Ginger Baker, Keith Moon—always used double-headed. That's the way the drums are *meant* to be recorded. But it's a little more complicated to fit it into the mix because you get unwanted frequencies. So, Donn took the heads off. *And* he forgot to mic the second kick drum. (I have two that I play in interdependent patterns. If you take one out it's like listening to a guitarist play with only half his strings!) *And,* most damning of all, Donn put *pillows in the drums!!*

You have to understand, the drummer always gets treated like dog meat. There's this bullshit idea that the drummer is just the timekeeper. The drum, my friends, is a voice—it's the only acoustic instrument on the record! The drum sound can really change the texture of the music you're making. But you're never going to get everything you want on your first shot. I drank a few more beers to take away the pain and then begrudgingly did whatever Donn wanted.

Ed told Donn and Ted he wanted to record his guitar exactly the way he played it onstage, with minimal overdubs. They were fine with whatever he needed to do to play the way they'd seen him when he performed. Donn told me when I saw him a few months ago that he remembers the first time he heard Ed make a mistake: "We were halfway through the first album, and in one song Ed went in one direction and Mike and everybody else went another and it was just a train wreck. I was sitting there with Ted in the control room and Ted looked over at me and said, 'I guess he's human after all.'"

By the end of the first day, we had recorded twenty-five songs, and we nailed most of them on the first take. "I over-dubbed the solo on only 'Runnin' with the Devil,' 'Ice Cream Man,' and 'Jamie's Cryin',' the rest are live," Ed said. "Because we were jumping around, drinking beer, and getting crazy, I think there's a vibe on the record."

For the very first sound on the record, the intro to "Runnin' with the Devil," the one that "sounds like a jet landing," as my brother described it to *Guitar Player*, "we took the horns out of all our cars—my brother's Opel, my old Volvo, ripped a couple out of a Mercedes and a Volkswagen—then mounted them in a box and hooked two car batteries to it and added a foot switch. We just used them as noisemakers before we got signed. Ted put it on tape, slowed it down, and then we came in with the bass." We loved that kind of thing. Smoke pots, car horns . . . everything DIY, which is another way of saying jerry-rigged. (Here's how Ed described his pedalboard to a journalist: "It's a piece of plywood with two controls for my Echoplex on it, an MXR Phase 90 that I've had for years, and an MXR flanger. They're all taped to a piece of board with black duct tape. And a lot of big-name players laugh themselves silly when they see it, but after they hear me, then they go, 'Can I plug in?'")

The second day was mostly vocals, getting the harmonies down. I wasn't there because I went to the Schick Center for the Control of Smoking and Weight. I knew I had to get healthy before the tour; it was obvious that it was going to be physically grueling. Schick was the soup du jour then—everyone who was anyone went there in the seventies to give up cigarettes or lose weight. (But not at the same time: they got me to quit smoking, but then I immediately gained forty pounds.) You went into this little room full of mountains of cigarette butts—smelled absolutely disgusting—and there were all these posters hanging on the walls picturing people with tracheotomies. There's a therapist on the other side of a pane of glass, and I remember telling her, "Listen, lady, I don't want you to talk about anything that isn't smoking. I am not walking out of here with an aversion to women or sex or *anything* other than cigarettes." And it worked.

While I was at Schick that day, they recorded "Happy Trails" at the studio, just as a kind of outtake. And there was a bigger problem: now Ted was worried about Dave's singing. Ted wrote in his book, "Dave's performance at Sunset Sound only raised my anxieties about his abilities." Ted was angling to have him replaced with Sammy Hagar, of all people, who he'd worked with on the Montrose albums.

We made it to that recording studio with Dave. And that meant we were leaving with him. You think we're going to spit him out as soon as we get where we've all been going? Dave wasn't the world's greatest singer, but he had everything else that we needed: the charisma, the physicality, the ego, the hair. And his lyrics were excellent—nobody gives him enough credit on this; I'm not sure even Dave knew how good they were. They were like Zen koans.

But beyond that, a band is like a gang: you've made a commitment to each other that you're going to do whatever it takes until you reach the end, and that provides the energy and the comradery to get you there. You share a sacred loyalty with your bandmates. (Did Dave return that loyalty later on down the line? That's another story. We'll get to it.) We told Ted that Van Halen was indivisible. Take it or leave it.

He took it, but he had Dave work with a vocal coach over the months that stretched out before our first tour.

THE LABEL TOLD US IT was time to stop playing the clubs; they wanted to have a big unveiling when we released the record. For about six months, they paid us $83.83 a month—where that number came from, I'll never know, but it wasn't even enough to cover beer. And we were used to hustling, so it felt really weird spending that much time doing nothing but playing pitch-and-putt golf and rehearsing in Dave's basement.

Of course, we also made our first record—*Van Halen*, the album that introduced our band to the world. But that only took two or three weeks. We had all the songs on our demo to choose from, and we already knew what we were doing, because we'd been playing together so much for so long. We wanted to sound on the record the way we sounded live, so we *recorded* live—as in, all of us in one room. It's an efficient way of doing things—a lot more efficient than, say, pulling the band and the sound apart by recording one instrument at a time and then putting them all back together in the mix, which is what most bands were doing at the time.

Dave had been working with his vocal coach and he had kind of cleaned himself up, not smoking cigarettes, eating healthy. The day we recorded "Jamie's Cryin'," Dave walked in and started singing, and Ted said, "Dave, it doesn't sound like you; it's not real." Ted told Dave to go and smoke something strong and eat something greasy. "I ate half a cheeseburger and drained a soda pop and smoked half a joint," Dave said. "Walked in, knocked out 'Jamie's Cryin'" in forty minutes."

Recording the entire album cost Warner Bros. $54,000. That's chump change for a label used to spending six or seven figures on a record. They got the deal of the century with Van Halen, in every respect.

"During that time, the songs came together just like that," Ted wrote. "Ed might play some new parts he'd written. I'd hear something I liked so I'd stop him and say, 'Hey, wait a second.' I'd dig into my notebook and say something like, 'Remember that descending riff from that shuffle tune? Let's put it right after this part you're working on now. What do you guys think?' Those guys almost always knew exactly what I was referencing. If Ed didn't remember, Al knew just how to jar his memory. Then we'd work on rearranging the song in question. After we'd get the new arrangement worked up, Dave would write an improved melody and often times update his lyrics. They had this ability to be modular with their songwriting, but they didn't even realize how well they did it." Hey, Ted, if you're reading this, thanks. But we knew!

The weird thing about Ted was that on the one hand he knew exactly what he had. "I wanted it to be perfect, but you know what? The humor came across. Ed's virtuosity came across. Al's power came across. Dave's smarts came across," Ted wrote. "That's the greatness of Van Halen." What I'm saying is that, in a way, Ted got us. But he also tried to push us toward commercial viability—which obviously was part of his job. "I wanted Van Halen sonically to have its heavy and dark aspects but at the same time, I wanted the band's pop sensibility to shine through," Ted wrote. "Their harmonies would be their secret weapon in this arena. When Mike and Ed sang together they sounded youthful, like the teenage sound of the early Beach Boys."

The problem was, that's not how *we* thought of ourselves. Words like "teenage" and "beach" had nothing to do with the sound we were going for. Led Zeppelin had some *heft* to it—that's what we wanted! The first time we took a tape out of Sunset Sound, Ed and I were horrified. It was so anti what we *were*.

"We were much heavier than what you heard on the record, and that's what Alex and I expected to hear," is how Ed put it. "I remember when Al and I went to Warner Bros. to pick up the cassettes of the first twenty-five-song demo tape we did for them. We popped it into the player in my van and expected to hear Led Zeppelin coming out, but we were kind of appalled by what we heard. It just didn't sound the way we wanted to sound. The first album sounds a little better, but it still wasn't the way we imagined it should sound. The drums sound small and you can barely hear the bass."

Obviously, Ed and I were completely on the same page about this. Don't forget: when we're done in the studio, we go home together. We discussed *everything*. And when it came to our sound, we pretty much agreed on everything.

But Ted did do something remarkable on our debut that I'll always be grateful for. He got "Eruption" on the record. That guitar solo alone is worth the price of admission. (*Now* you're on the Zeppelin level—they had a solo on their record. Remember "Heartbreaker"?) And the whole thing happened by accident. "'Eruption' wasn't really planned to be on the record," Ed remembered. "Al and me were messing around rehearsing for a show we had to do at the Whisky. I was warming up, doing my solo, Ted walks in and says, 'Hey, what's that? . . . It's great! Let's put it on the record.'" Anyone who knows anything about guitar would understand that Ed was exceptional from listening to *any* track on *Van Halen*. But "Eruption" showcased his ingenuity—it was like the summation of everything he'd been working on and obsessed with since he first picked up my Teisco.

Steve Lukather of Toto, who was a good friend of Ed's for over forty years, had a vivid way of describing what that solo did to him when he first heard it, before we'd ever met him: "We were all going, 'What the fuck? What is that? How do you do that?' It was a game changer. I felt my penis shrink, because I was thinking about what I was going to do on *my* solo." HA!

Being creative, you have your own vision, but you also have to convince others of that vision, and it can be a monumental task. Ted did that for us with "Eruption." The record company doesn't want that shit. They're thinking: How are people supposed to dance to a guitar solo? How are they going to get *that* on the radio? Ted knew it didn't matter. "Eruption" was just so mind-blowing it broke every rule, exceeded every expectation. You have to be blind not to hear it.

"For my money, Van Halen is the first significant new kid on the block," Jimmy Page said when he heard it. "Very dazzling."

Unfortunately, Ed's genius didn't extend to foresight. Not long after we recorded, Ed just had to play a tape of our new songs for Barry Brandt backstage at the Whisky one night. Well, surprise surprise, a week later we hear that Barry's band Angel is in the studio recording their own cover of "You Really Got Me," a Kinks song we'd played in the clubs and had recorded for the album. Warner Bros. doesn't want another band coming out with a cover of the same song at the same time as us, so they decide the only thing to do is release our version as the album's first single. Nice going, Ed! Now the people who don't know us are going to have their first Van Halen experience on the radio with a song that isn't even by Van Halen. That wasn't exactly what I'd had in mind.

"YOU SHOULD SEE THE FIRST album cover Warner Bros. designed for us," my brother once said. "They tried to make us look like the Clash." You can see it online and there are still some EPs floating around with that art on the jacket. It was all wrong; didn't capture our essence: Mikey is wearing white pants, for God's sake, and he looks like he's about to burst into tears. Dave is next to him with his eyes closed. *I'm* front and center, in the foreground, looking like I'm about to get in a fight, and Ed's kind of behind me, to my left, with his arms folded in front of his chest, all pissed off. We didn't look like we were there to bring the party, we looked like we were there to report for detention!

Dave in particular couldn't stand it. He said it was because our name was too small (which was true) and because the look was too punk (which was also true), and that that was his issue with it—which was total BS. Dave didn't like it because he wasn't out in front!

Warner Bros. didn't want the band to be miserable right out of the gate, so they hired Elliot Gilbert to shoot us playing at the Whisky instead. Those pictures became the cover everyone knows. I'm just a blur; you can't see me at all behind my drum kit. But I liked that all four of us were presented as equals: four quadrants of the album cover that add up to the whole, all of us in motion in a kind of hot fog. I liked that Ed was smiling like a maniac and that his guitar—a soon-to-be-famous Frankenstrat—was so prominent in the shot. (There were bike reflectors glued to the back of that guitar so it could throw light around onstage. The front pickup was purely ornamental, there to fill a hole Ed had made.) I liked the way we all glowed in the dark like we were radioactive or about to go up in flames. It gave you some sense of what we were like live: smoking.

A designer named Dave Bhang drew up the Van Halen logo that became famous: the winged VH that was smack in the middle of the first record, unforgettable. I liked that the wings were an implicit nod to the Led Zeppelin Icarus image, because they were our favorite band, but also because they suggested the idea of a human being striving to fly—getting too close to the sun but giving it everything he has to reach the heights. All of that appealed to me and felt right for the band.

In Ed's telling, we "put it on the album so that it would be clear that we had nothing to do with the punk movement. It was our way of saying 'Hey, we're just a fucking rock 'n' roll band, don't try to slot us with the Sex Pistols thing just because it's becoming popular.'" You can't blame Warner Bros. for trying to fit us into a niche—that's their job. But Van Halen was too joyful, had too much of a sense of humor, to be rammed in with punk. I guess you could argue the Ramones were funny, and we played at a gig they headlined at the Golden West in the spring of '77 billed as a "Punk Rock Ballroom Blitz." We enjoyed their spirit, but part of the ethos of punk was this anti-elitism that extended to musicianship, and we couldn't relate to that at all. We weren't just a couple of guys banging on instruments; we were real players, and that was the most important thing to us. You're not going to find a punk band like that. We were too original and too musical. And we had too much respect for classic rock.

That's what we loved and that's what had earned us so many really passionate fans. Before we went out on tour, we had a farewell show at the Pasadena Civic Auditorium. "The whole crowd was pumping their fists," Ted remembers. "It was like I was at a Beatles concert in the middle of Pasadena, and they didn't even have a record out yet."

In January 1978 Warner Bros. released five of the new Van Halen songs to radio stations pressed on red vinyl. (On the front of the sleeve was our logo; on the back was Elmer Fudd, another Warner Bros. star.) One night shortly before we left on tour, I'm asleep in bed and Ed comes screaming in at two in the morning: we're on the radio. At that moment, I didn't much care that we were playing a Kinks cover. All I could hear was *us*—my brother, me, and the guys, screaming our song out over the airwaves.

Just like we'd always dreamed.

WE WERE ON THE ROAD for eleven months straight.

In the late seventies, touring was not the organized machine it is now—rock 'n' roll itself was still relatively new. We used our friends from Pasadena to make up our main crew. My buddy Gregg Emerson from high school became my drum tech. The guitar tech was Ed's friend Rudy Leiren, who also became our announcer: "Ladies and gentlemen, the mighty Van Halen!" For Mikey's tech, Noel Monk brought in Gary Geller, who everyone called Big Red because of his red hair. These were our friends, so we did have to sit them down and say, "Listen: you're working for us now." It was an issue sometimes with Gregg, who was used to thinking of Ed as younger than us, someone he could push around, like his own little brother. We all intermingled. The bus driver's wife became the wardrobe person. For better or worse, I took over driving the truck at various points, and Ed at others.

Our first stop was Chicago, February 28, 1978. At that point our album had been out less than three weeks. Warner Bros. made us the opening act on a triple bill with Ronnie Montrose and Journey, just after Steve Perry became their lead singer. They were all great players if not really our cup of tea. You couldn't have gotten less rock 'n' roll; I don't know that we were really an easy sell to Journey's fans. But the way we saw it, we had to convince the whole world we'd arrived. Those audiences were as good a place to start as any. We rehearsed for a few days and then it was time for the first show of our first tour in front of five thousand people at the Aragon Ballroom.

We almost missed it because we got stuck in a traffic jam. But Big Red was driving that day and he took it upon himself to bypass the jam by cruising the last few blocks to the Aragon up on the sidewalk.

I'll never forget how cramped and dim and freezing cold and lifeless the dressing room was there. All those old buildings are like that, remnants of the past. They were supposed to provide beer and towels, but there were only four skimpy rags and one six-pack. For all of us. Well, that ain't going to cut it. My own personal needs alone were probably double that.

We were used to crummy surroundings, but we weren't expecting it here. (I *really* don't like the cold. I'm from California!) Also, there wasn't enough room for all three bands' equipment, so basically you put the headliner's—Journey's—stuff at the back of the stage, then Ronnie Montrose's, and then we get whatever's left at the very front to set up and play. After each band performs, their equipment gets pushed off to the side, so that the act that follows them has more space. That's fine for them, but for us it meant we only had about a dozen-foot-wide stage to work with—and our physicality was a big part of our show. Keep in mind, I had a *massive* drum kit. Dave and I always agreed it had to look the way it sounded: huge! It barely fit on the stage.

Obviously, it was all exciting. Within a month of its release, *Van Halen* was number nineteen on the US charts. And I loved touring at that point in my life; so did Ed. It's a pretty ideal life for a young man who just wants to play music, meet women, and party. You meet new people, you're out there in the mix. People are 99 percent the same wherever you go, and we figured that out fast. They just want to have a good time, and it's our job to give them one.

Ed and I always took the back of the bus; honestly it wasn't that much tighter than the living conditions we were used to. We had these cots that kind of pulled down from off the wall. And we had each other back there—we could talk, we could make music, we could drink Schlitz, we could do whatever we wanted. We had to be strategic about our drinking, though, because we knew we had an obligation to the audience: they've paid good money and we have to give them our all every night. We never wanted to be too drunk—or too hungover—to play our best. It was a delicate balance.

We were also young and stupid. I remember getting to a venue somewhere in New England where the food they gave us was really terrible. And keep in mind, when we're on tour, backstage and the back of the bus are our *home*. You can't give us this junk! So we started chucking the food at the wall, up onto the ceiling, you name it. Pretty soon it gets out of hand and there's food everywhere and broken trays and so on. Long story short, after the gig they retaliated by setting part of the building on fire and trying to frame us for arson.

There was another time when Dave threw a television out of our hotel window. There's no excuse; we were just bored or drunk or amped up or all three things at once. Understandably, the guy at the front desk called the cops when he saw a TV go whizzing through the air outside his window. But by the time the police got to us we'd gone and snagged a TV from a different room and put it in Dave's, so all we had to do was look innocent and respectable when they came to our door. I'm not saying that was easy.

While we were behaving like degenerates, our record was climbing the charts. "We're kickin' some ass," Ed bragged to Jas Obrecht, a journalist from *Guitar World* who was only a year or two older than Ed. They met shooting hoops backstage before a gig in the spring of '78 and stayed in touch; Ed talked to him often over the years. (That first time, Obrecht had actually come to interview Pat Travers, who blew him off, so he ended up interviewing my brother instead . . . worked out well for everyone except Travers.) "When we started out with Montrose and Journey, we were brand-new; I think our album was only out a week at the start of the tour. And now we're almost passing up Journey on the charts and stuff. So they're freakin' out. I think they might be happy to get rid of us. We're very energetic and we get up there and blaze on the people for thirty minutes—that's all we're allowed to play," Ed continued. "We don't get sound checks; we don't get shit. But we're still blazing on the people, man. We're getting a strong encore every night."

I WAS INTO ARTHUR BROWN, the guy who sang "Fire" and wore a pair of flaming horns. So I started lighting my drums on fire onstage. It's a cheap gag; all you need is a mallet that you soak in lighter fluid. There are better, safer, fancier ways of doing it with a gas jet, and we got to that later, but in 1978, we were a bare-bones operation. I traveled everywhere with the gear for my pyrotechnics. When we got to Schaumburg, Illinois, there were all these tires lying around near our hotel and I started thinking, *Wouldn't it be fun to light them on fire?* And of course I had my pyro bag right there with me. (Fire was a really big part of my life.) Anyway, I'm sitting there with a lighter and a burning tire and a cop materializes with his gun drawn. This is not good. This is one of those instances where Noel Monk was good at getting us out of trouble.

"When you are on the road with a young and hungry rock band on the cusp of stardom, the usual rules of decorum that one adheres to in polite society simply do not exist," as Noel put it in his book *Runnin' with the Devil*. "Spend six months on the road, sleep in buses and hotels, perform a hundred shows before drunk and adoring crowds, and see what happens to your moral compass. Things just get . . . twisted."

Pranks and mildly destructive behavior just naturally sneak into the equation if you're a guy in your twenties in a rock band on the road. Stupid stuff like ramming firecrackers into hollow towel rods and setting off these rockets out our hotel room window. (And woe to the window that "doesn't open." Dave traveled with a wrench.) Deranged science experiments are somehow an essential element of touring. "What happens when you jump on a toilet? What can we expect when you disassemble a sink? What happens if we do both at the same time in the same bathroom?" Dave wrote in his book. Ah, the study of hydraulics! "It's part of engineering, it's part of bridge building, heavy construction, and it's a very important part of rock 'n' roll on the road."

When you're spending every night playing songs about letting the whole human animal out of its cage—the essence of rock 'n' roll—it's pretty hard to get the beast back behind bars the next day. So we were always trying to outdo each other avenging the last prank. I can't remember when it first started, but a major element of life on the road on an early Van Halen tour was getting "fished"—which is to say opening your guitar case or your sock drawer or whatever and finding a frozen fish staring back at you. The dead creature had been deposited there by your bandmate or a member of your crew while your back was turned. I've never laughed as hard in my life as I used to laugh when someone got fished, even if that someone was me. It was something of a matter of pride. "It's an honor, knowing that all eyes are upon you, watching your reaction, to see if you're suitably passionate and dramatic," as Dave put it. "Getting fished is no time for meditational acceptance. Let's see some fury! We went out of our way to fish you, now let's have some reaction. And of course the optimal—being an offensive player—is being able to solicit retribution, to know that you've fished so well that there's going to be some payback, and that gives you something to look forward to. Now you've got something to think about on the bus, knowing the hunter is now the hunted."

We didn't invent this kind of behavior. Look at Keith Moon! He was the drummer for the Who, and the night he turned twenty-one, he's partying at the pool of the Holiday Inn in Flint, Michigan, with the guys from Herman's Hermits, who they were touring with. They get in a birthday cake fight. (We had tons of cake fights on the road. Never give a cake to a drunk young rock musician.) Everyone is covered in frosting, slipping around, things are getting wilder and wilder, and they start throwing beer bottles into the pool. But Moon takes it to the next level. Someone's Lincoln Continental was parked right by them; he gets in, takes off the handbrake, and steers the thing straight into the swimming pool. ("And the water was pouring in—coming in through the bloody pedal holes in the floorboard, squirting in through the windows," Moon said in '72. "I'm sitting there, thinking about me situation, as the water creeps up to me nose." His bandmate John Entwistle said this never happened, but I'm team Moon all the way. First of all, he's a drummer, and more important, never let the truth get in the way of a good story.)

Somewhere in Massachusetts, Dave and I were getting picked up, supposedly in a limousine. Instead, this kid comes to get us in a Cadillac Seville. Well, we thought that was outrageous.

Once we're in, Dave starts yanking on the car's ceiling until the headliner comes off. Before you know it, we're all tearing the car apart. By the time we got to the gig the driver was practically in tears. Unfortunately for us, it turned out that the driver happened to be the promoter's son. And the Cadillac happened to be the promoter's car.

Look, you're living on a lot of McDonald's. (Filet-O-Fish was my go-to; Ed's was a Big Mac.) You have no control over what you're eating beyond that. At the end of each gig you throw your wet clothes in the road case, and that goes in the truck overnight. Next day you go to get dressed and everything is frozen. You grin and bear it. You get tough. It's not the same as being in the army, but it's also not what you would do by choice, and over time you become a road warrior. You start treating your surroundings the way the road is treating you.

"Manners flew out the window—along with tables, chairs, lamps, and anything else that was of little obvious use and had the misfortune not to be nailed down. I had been with other bands that had trashed their surroundings, but they had nothing on Van Halen," Noel wrote—which is bullshit, Noel had toured with the Sex Pistols. "It was all part of the process of becoming a tried-and-tested rock star; understanding that you could do almost anything, and ignoring the switch that stops you from doing it. David seemed to understand that from the beginning, and embraced it wholeheartedly, in part because he so desperately wanted to be a star."

Sure. There's all that. But there's a simpler explanation for why we partied so hard and behaved so badly and got with as many girls as we could get our hands on: we were young. "It was our first tour. It was 1978. We were doing anything and everything we ever read about and then some," as my brother put it. Remember being twenty-one, twenty-two? It's not the peak of your powers of judgment. I was wearing a studded black leather jumpsuit on-stage, for crying out loud.

What I'm saying is, whether we knew it or not, we were still kids. Every night of that tour we called home to talk to our dad.

INTERLUDE

I think that's about when our childhoods finally ended.

In a way, we grew up fast, Ed. We started working young; we started drinking young. Before our respective ages had even reached double digits, we'd already become fluent in a second language and a new culture. But looking back now, with the benefit of hindsight—but without the benefit of my brother by my side—I see that we were still very young and, in a way, still innocent when we put out our first record.

We didn't know the music business. We didn't know what it was to be married men, let alone fathers. We didn't know that our bodies wouldn't always bounce right back from being filled with whatever substance we threw into them—that all the months that turned into years of pushing as hard as we could, never sleeping, never staying in the same place for long, eating fast food on the road, would catch up with us.

At the time it seemed great. You remember how freeing it was to wake up in the back of that bus and find the sun rising over a new city? The slate is wiped clean and you're reborn in every place—you've got a whole new shot at life! Sure, wherever you go, there you are, and so on, but for the audience it's a whole new you. The gig in San Antonio wasn't up to snuff? Nobody knows that in Albuquerque. It was like the day before never happened.

This was before the internet, of course, so everyone was just there, in the moment. You didn't look out at the audience and see a million cell phones held in the air recording you. You just saw a sea of people partying—and any number of the female partygoers without their shirts on! In a way, I wish we had more videos of our early years, because I'd love to watch them now. But you never could have captured what it was really like—the energy, the sweat, the smell, the crowd, the sound.

I think we were always aware that you reach your creative peak in youth. You're only going to be at the top of your game for a finite amount of time. Then, if you're lucky, you spend the rest of your career going through what you did when you were at your best, tweaking it, repeating it, riffing on it. We knew that when we were young. But I think you lost sight of it later in life.

I fantasize about an alternate reality where you didn't torture yourself to your dying day thinking you had to re-create the feeling and the output you had in your twenties.

Dad always told us, you have to have your own sound—when you hear the first few bars of any Van Halen song, you better know you're hearing Van Halen. We achieved that. It's something to be proud of. André Gide said that "art is a collaboration between God and the artist, and the less the artist does the better." I guess God had a good idea for a Van Halen sound, and we were pretty good at transmitting it to the audience. What an honor—what a pleasure! There's nothing I'd rather have spent my life doing.

But looking back on it, it doesn't mean as much to me without you here to share it.

NINE

When we toured the UK for the first time, we were no longer traveling with bands whose music didn't speak to us. We were opening for Black Sabbath.

It's hard to overstate what this meant to us. We worshipped Sabbath. We'd been playing their music since we were kids. We wanted to name our band after one of their songs! "I remember sitting down in front of the stereo with the needle on the record with Edward trying to get the words from 'Iron Man' so we could play it at a backyard party," my roadie Gregg told some documentarians. "Next thing you know, here we are opening up. We got our gear put away very quickly when we were touring with them because we all wanted to watch their concert."

I remember the first night of our tour with them, after we finished our set, sitting down in the basement of the arena when Sabbath came on. Hearing them start playing, it really hit me. We were sharing a stage with our idols.

There was a problem, though. I noticed when we played that night—and I kept on noticing—that there was not a girl in sight. The Sabbath fans were almost entirely male, and almost entirely dressed in black T-shirts. I remember saying to Dave, "I love rock 'n' roll, but where the women be?"

That was our only grievance. Their crowds were great to us. "Van Halen was utterly fearless and tireless each time they took the stage. And it was fascinating to see the band's confidence grow. They didn't give a shit that they were playing in front of Black Sabbath die-hards," Noel wrote in his book. He's wrong, though. We cared plenty. "They scared the shit out of us," Ed admitted. To us, Sabbath was the ultimate. It mattered how we sounded to Sabbath fans because we *were* Sabbath fans. But Noel was right about this: "By the time Edward finished his solo in 'Eruption' he had them eating out of the palm of his hand."

We did twenty-five shows with Sabbath in thirty days. They had been at this for ten years and were a hell of a lot closer to middle age than we were, so if the schedule was grueling for us, it must have been epic for them. Of course, they were traveling in a tricked-out tour bus and we were in a shitmobile that didn't have any beds . . . we slept sitting up every night we were on the road. (I remember the driver's name was Keith and he'd say, "I take care of the coach and the coach takes care of me!") It was our first tour, and though we didn't know it at the time, it was Sabbath's last.

"Black Sabbath was the clear headliner on this tour but Van Halen stole the show," Noel wrote about that tour. "They were young and vital and filled with the sort of energy and ambition that had begun to drain from Sabbath." I'd never want to say a negative word about Sabbath—to us they were gods to worship. But even they saw it that way. "Van Halen blew us off the stage every night," Ozzy said in the press years later. "They kicked our asses. But it convinced me of two things. My days with Sabbath were over. And Van Halen was going to be a very successful band."

Boat ride from Holland to America, 1962. Notice the little
dark-haired girl at the end of the table—I thought I had more than a week!

Where it all started.
Eugenia and
Jan Van Halen on
their wedding day.

The master. Without my father's teaching, we wouldn't have been anywhere. This photo was probably taken when he was in the service.

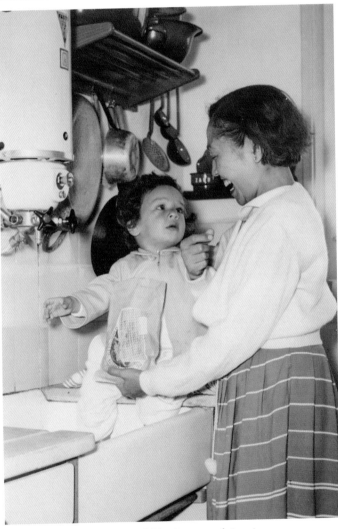

My mom and I having a good time in the kitchen in Nijmegen . . . next to the hot-water heater that almost killed me.

Me and my dad at the arboretum in Arcadia, not long after our arrival in California. I'd never seen a cactus before—not in real life, anyway. And I'd never seen a wide-open expanse like that back in Holland. It all seemed so surreal.

My first school picture. I was everything my mother ever wanted.

Ed and Mom on their way to a piano contest. The anxiety started six months before the event. And Ed had his music with him, which he couldn't read!

Our dad was in the air force. Guns and the military were
part of our DNA. And I already loved vehicles.

Ed and Dad at the arboretum.

Our band, the Trojan Rubber Company, in 1971.
("Smoking aids in digestion," they used to tell us.)

Second tour. We heard about the Edgewater Hyatt in Seattle from Zeppelin—you could go fishing right out of your window. And we wouldn't stop until we caught something.

Ed was lucky he was thin—everything fit him.

Mr. Charles let me graduate
despite the *Bull Sheet*, in 1969.
Ed was two years behind me.

We weren't aware of stealing the spotlight from them at the time. We were more concerned about what they thought of *us*—whether we measured up. I mean, they truly were legends. And it was amazing to see the comradery when we went to the pubs with them. Everyone treated them like they were just regular guys from around the way, and that's how they acted. The distinctions dissolved and we all felt equal. It was beautiful.

Tony Iommi was our kind of guy. When he was seventeen, Tony lost the tips of two fingers while he was working at a sheet metal factory. He was already a passionate guitarist by then. A lesser man would have just given it up: how are you supposed to play the guitar without the ends of the middle and ring fingers of your right hand—your *fretting* hand? He was just a stubborn, resilient motherfucker, like my dad, who wouldn't take no for an answer. Tony figured out a way. He had prosthetic tips fabricated and he became one of the great guitarists of his generation playing with those fake fingers. Impressive, right?

We all respected the hell out of him. But guitarists just naturally gravitate to each other, and Tony and Ed became lifelong friends. "I'd never heard anything like it . . . like, 'Bloody hell, what's this?'" Tony said of Ed's playing. "We really got to know each other well on that tour. Ed used to come around to my room most nights after the show. Or I'd go around to his room and we'd sit there talking. We used to have such a great time together. We really spilt our hearts out with each other," Tony continued, "we had a lot in common." Neither of them ever learned to read music. Tony and Ed were both innovators who liked to tweak their equipment. And they just got a kick out of each other both as people and as players—they were truly mutual fans. "Nobody can play like him," Tony told *Rolling Stone* right after my brother passed. "I can't stop thinking about it, to be honest . . . It's very, very sad."

Ozzy Osbourne was a real everyman under all that eyeliner—a regular guy's guy. He was great to us. He invited us to his house in the countryside outside of Birmingham—one of the trappings of being a successful rock entity. It was like a storybook English country house, a little lake in the backyard with all these duck decoys floating in it. We're sitting there having a relaxing day, not talking business or anything because the workload was pretty intense, so when you got a day off, God knows you took it. Anyway, we're having a few out in the yard, and out of the blue Ozzy gets up and walks into the house, and when he comes out he's got a shotgun. And we're all just pretending like we're not seeing this; we're not going to comment. Well, he picks up his gun and starts shooting up those duck decoys, blowing them away one by one.

We were all stunned. Nobody said a word. Oz walks back into the house, puts the shotgun away, and comes back out again like nothing happened. It was like fucking performance art. I love that man.

The next morning when the family wakes up, Sharon brings the kids over to Ozzy, passed out on the couch: time to kiss Daddy good night.

We found out our album went gold while we were in Aberdeen, Scotland. We went completely nuts. We were staying at a really upscale hotel—I remember there were lots of golfers there, lots of plaid. I can't really offer you any kind of logical explanation for this (other than the fact that we discovered Glenmorangie Scotch the same night we discovered we had our first gold record), but we completely trashed our hotel room . . . just made a total mess of it, celebrating and throwing things around, getting in an epic fire-extinguisher battle. (I know: it was our response to everything. Bad food? Trash the hotel room. Amazing news? Trash the hotel room. What can I say? We did not quite grasp that though Warner Bros. was "paying" the bill for everything that happened on the road, they were paying it out of our earnings. More on this later.)

We soon found out that Aberdeen is not a good place to get out of line. The hotel called the police, and when they showed up, members of our crew were frantically flushing their drugs down the toilet on the bus . . . not realizing there's no actual *plumbing* on the bus: if you throw your drugs in that toilet, they're all still there for the police to find; all you've done is made your drugs disgusting and unusable if the police happen to miss them.

Fortunately—for us and for them—the cops didn't dig around in that toilet. But they did escort us to the airport, where they told us in no uncertain terms, "Do not come back here ever again." And to the best of my knowledge, we didn't.

WE KEPT TOURING WITH SABBATH in the United States, which was great for us because it meant we got to play arenas, which we wouldn't have been able to fill on our own at that point. It also meant we got to keep hanging out with the guys in Sabbath, and that was a blast. We did a *lot* of drinking together. I guess Dave and Ozzy did a ton of blow together on that tour, too, but I wasn't a part of that. I was hyper to begin with—I needed alcohol to slow me down. (I did coke *once*, years later, at Ed's recording studio, 5150, and for some reason I got this overwhelming urge to stand up on the console and I really could have destroyed the thing. It wasn't pretty. When it was over, I remember Ed getting this real sweet look on his face and going, "Al, please promise me you'll never do it again." I told him, "Okay.")

We played Summerfest in front of fifty-six thousand people at Anaheim Stadium with Sabbath and the band Boston (if you're young you may not even remember them, but they were huge at the time—Boston had one of the bestselling debut albums in history when it dropped in '76, and their song "More Than a Feeling" was everywhere; you could not get away from it). Opening for those two bands was huge, and Dave got it in his head that we needed to make a grand entrance. (Who opened for us? A guy you've probably never heard of. I think his name was Sammy Hagar . . .)

It was inspired: we got four skydivers with shaggy hair not that different from our own to jump out of a plane over the stadium as the announcer called out, "From out of the sky, Van Halen is coming into the stadium!" Everyone is screaming like crazy, the parachutes burst open as the skydivers zig and zag in the air so as to make the whole thing as dramatic as humanly possible, and then they land in the parking lot behind the stage, where we leap out of hiding wearing skydiver suits so everyone thinks we're these amazing daredevils willing to risk our lives for a good show. The skydivers made it through the stunt fine. I, on the other hand, managed to twist my ankle tripping over a cable on the way onto the stage before tens of thousands of screaming fans. I was howling with equal parts elation and agony as I peeled off my ornamental parachute and climbed up the drum riser.

Our parents came to see us do our gig in Houston, Texas. What I vividly remember is my mom coming backstage afterward and taking a look at all the girls who were kind of buzzing around. She turned to me and said, "What are you doing with all these *wie wils?*"—that's Dutch for, basically, girls who want to. "I thought you had better taste." (Nope.) She also said, "Alex, drink a glass of milk in between those twenty-five beers." Clearly, the road was no place for her.

One afternoon in Nashville, we went to do our sound check and suddenly everyone was going, "Where the hell is Ozzy?" And pretty quickly the vibe gets a little edgy. Like, Jesus, maybe somebody kidnapped him. Though it didn't actually represent them, Black Sabbath played heavily off all that devil imagery; maybe people weren't so amused by that down there in the Bible Belt. We were completely freaked out. You didn't have the internet then, so you'd get everything in fragments; information trickled in and you never had any idea what was actually going on.

We all spent the night looking for Ozzy, checking every stairwell, until about two in the morning, and then we went to bed worried as hell. Next day at breakfast, who comes waltzing into the hotel restaurant like he doesn't have a care in the world but Ozzy Osbourne. He'd been asleep for almost two days. And was completely unaware of it. He was like a heavy metal Rip van Winkle.

See, we'd been staying at a series of Sheratons, and when we arrived at our hotel in Nashville the previous morning, Ozzy had just looked at the key in his pocket—from the night *before*, when we were at a *different* Sheraton or Hilton—and gone to the room number on that key. When he got there, as luck would have it there was a maid cleaning the room, and she let him in and went on her merry way. He went to sleep and the rest is history.

It was funny as hell and we were all obviously relieved he was okay. Sure, Oz was probably worn out from days—and nights—of doing blow with Dave instead of sleeping. They even had a name for it: they called it the "krell wars" because Dave always called cocaine "krell." (The Krell were these aliens in the movie *Forbidden Planet*, and they were really advanced. I guess Dave felt like one of them when he was coked up.) But really it could have happened to any of us: we were *beat* when we weren't onstage. When you're not performing, you're trying to sleep on a bus, you never get a moment to yourself, you're always doing some press or promotion, and then you need time for drinking and things of that nature. All kidding aside, they run you into the ground on those tours.

We were less than thrilled to do the makeup show the promoter required after Sabbath missed their gig that night Ozzy took his extra-long nap. Not only did it mean losing one of our very few days off, they rescheduled us for *noon*. Noon is not a great time to play rock 'n' roll.

"Van Halen stole the spotlight from Sabbath every night . . . that sort of upstaging almost never happens," Noel wrote. "Why this didn't destroy the rapport between the two bands over the course of a two-leg tour . . . is something of a mystery."

Not really. I think it's pretty simple. Musicians who love what they do and take it seriously—live for it—respect each other as kindred spirits. We didn't think of it as upstaging anyone. We thought we were paying homage to the people who came before us, who inspired us, and who showed us the way. That's how you learn how to live, how to be.

OUR FIRST TIME BACK IN Amsterdam since leaving as kids was on that tour, when we visited Northern Europe. The Iron Curtain was still up; all the Eastern Bloc countries were off-limits. But we made it back to Holland, the place where it all started for us.

Of course, we get to Amsterdam and the first thing everyone wants to do is head straight for the red-light district. That's for the tourists, not the locals! I'll never understand the novelty of hookers in shop windows. Guys, it's the world's oldest profession: there's nothing new here. But we took them around and they all thought they'd been to the magic kingdom.

We were playing at the Paradiso Theater, and my first reaction when we got there was, *Seriously? You call this paradise? This is supposed to be our triumphant return. And we're playing in this place?* Old building, nothing special. Compared to some of the really great theaters in Europe where we'd been, it was lame.

Maybe ten members of our extended family came to the gig, from both my mom's and dad's sides. I remember Ed and I felt stressed out by the whole thing. We were worried about meeting family obligations and playing our best and doing all the Dutch press, and it was all a little overwhelming.

Generally, I liked the adventure of these new places and different cultures, but I think Ed missed the comfort of his tiny room, where he knew every inch and didn't have to think about anything but his guitar. It's like he needed a compressed, familiar environment to let his mind get really loose and creative, which is the only thing that made him totally content.

We had a guitar tech from Argentina on that tour, a guy named José Arredondo, wonderful man. (I remember one of his jokes: "Hey, Alex, when I got married I thought my wife was a nun." "Why's that, José?" "Because I got nun in the morning, nun in the afternoon, and nun at night!" Something in his delivery made that work, I swear.) José had worked for the Stones, so he had a pedigree, and that made us take what he said more seriously, listen to him more intently.

He convinced Ed that he should build his own amp. If we had any time between traveling and sound checks and performing, Ed wanted to spend it going to music stores wherever we were to see if they had anything that he could chop up and repurpose to get his equipment a little closer to the sound he wanted, the sound José had convinced him he could attain if he just took his Frankenstein-ing to the next level. "If I hear a sound in my head," Ed has said, "I will stop at nothing to achieve it." It's the truth, and it nearly drove him crazy—sometimes it nearly drove me crazy, too.

We could go wherever we wanted to shop, drink, eat, because we were still almost completely unknown. There was one gig at a convention center, I can't remember where, when Ed went out to get a guitar he'd left on the bus and they wouldn't let him back inside. It was our only tour like that.

Europe is pretty much all the same from the back of a tour bus. The sensibilities and the language change from country to country, but at least from our way of looking at it, out the window of a bus or from up onstage, you could be in Belgium and you wouldn't know it wasn't Holland unless you saw the flag. "All those years of playing, practically for free, in front of inebriated, screaming fans, either in backyards or steamy clubs, had made the band not just incredibly tight and efficient but utterly fearless. You could throw Van Halen into almost any venue, in front of any crowd, and they would simply do their thing," Noel observed. "So they weren't in-timidated by Le Théâtre Mogador or by the prospect of playing in front of French fans for the very first time. On some level, it was just another night and another gig." He's right. We weren't jaded, we were just professional. My father taught us: do your *job*.

When we got to Japan it was like visiting another planet. We couldn't understand a word anyone said—which was great,

I loved it. When you can't speak a language, you find other commonalities with people and it can actually be a more in-depth way of communicating. Japan in 1978 had not been polluted by Western capitalism yet—there was only one McDonald's, no CNN, nothing. Unfortunately, we came shortly after an incident when some concertgoers were trampled to death at a performance by a band called Ritchie Blackmore's Rainbow. For a while there, Japan wasn't allowing any rock shows at all. The government ultimately softened their position, and we were able to play, but everyone had to remain seated, we were told, or they'd stop the gig. It was like: sit down; shut up; listen. Really weird way to do rock 'n' roll. It felt like our old piano recitals where you could hear a pin drop.

What more than made up for that was that when I got back to my hotel room one night, I found a surprise waiting for me: there were two very attractive, barely dressed Japanese girls in my closet. I wasn't going to leave them in there alone—it would have been rude.

So that was great. What was less fun was when one of their fathers showed up at the hotel the next day—with a sword. I'm not making this up. He told me I had damaged his family honor and the only way I could restore it was by marrying his daughter. We were in a totally foreign culture; I had no idea what the rules were. I'm looking at our itinerary thinking, *When are we out of here?* Fortunately for the girl, we were gone before her father could arrange a shotgun wedding—a samurai sword wedding, in this case.

The greatest thing was finding out that wherever you went in the world, all you had to do was set up your gear and start playing and you could get people partying. That was an amazing feeling.

You know you're bringing it—it doesn't matter where you go. It doesn't matter that you can't speak the language, because music is universal. So is youth.

IT WAS ON THE JAPANESE leg of the tour that we realized that while Marshall Berle was a funny guy, he did not have what it took to get Van Halen as far as we intended to go. We had a meeting set up with some people who wanted to film us and we needed to negotiate an arrangement. We get to the meeting, and it's in this immaculate boardroom—you didn't want to touch anything because the table was so clean and shiny; you were afraid to take a step on that spotless carpet. The first thing out of Marshall's mouth to the assembled Japanese gentlemen was, "Okay, I know you guys make good stereos, give me a couple of those." We were appalled. Jesus, Marshall: first let's set up this thing with them filming us!

Which brings us to Marshall's bigger sin. *He* was filming us, all the time. So far, no problem. He had this Super 8 camera, and whenever he showed up to see us on the road, he'd be filming whatever was going on, which included a certain amount of sex and drugs as well as rock 'n' roll. Again, no problem. But it *became* a problem when Marshall, for reasons known only to him, thought it would be a good idea to show his footage to everyone at Warner Bros.

I guess he was trying to impress people there with how plugged in he was to the wildness of life on the road? It's impossible to say. Point is, it showed us Marshall had no judgment in terms of what was appropriate, or in the band's best interest. We told him we were moving on.

Incidentally, I have no hard feelings against the guy—I saw Marshall the last time I was in Florida, where he lives now. He still makes me laugh. Marshall just wasn't the right guy to get us where we knew we were headed.

The problem with hiring the so-called right guys: they might know what they're doing with business, but you can bet they're going to siphon off a solid chunk of what ought to be yours. So you think, *I'll just hire myself.* But then you're going to lose what he would have stolen from you anyway, because you have no idea how anything works!

Dave in particular liked to be in control of every little detail. I think his dad told him, "When you have a business, you need to know every aspect of it." Dave misinterpreted that to mean you have to *micromanage* every aspect of it, whether you know anything about it or not. (You don't have to take my word for it, take his: "Right from the start with Van Halen programs and T-shirts and such that went on the road, we hired out to other companies, but I presided over all of it, approved everything. Got involved in every level. Not just, 'Oh, here we finished all the layout and it's done and here it is, what do you think?' But approving the layout acetates, color tones, picking color patches, and on and on." "On and on" are the operative words: he drove everyone *crazy*.) But it wasn't only Dave, to be fair; we were all young and brash and we figured, sure, we'll make mistakes, but at least we'll put the money where *we* think it's right for *our* career. And we tried. But no: there aren't enough hours in a day to book the band and promote the band and merchandise the band and *be* the band.

So, with Dave's prodding, we promoted Noel Monk from road manager to real manager. We told him there were two conditions: he had to wear a suit, and with that suit he had to wear . . . an eye patch. Noel thought about it for a second and replied, "Okay. Which eye?"

He was fun to have around. Noel was very into guns and security—his idea of a good read was *Soldier of Fortune* magazine; he knew nine different ways to kill a person using just his pinkies. I remember going to see his new house with Ed and our dad one day, and he had *airlocks* separating different sections of the place in case he ever had an intruder. Then he had this massive fortress of a wall safe, and he showed it to us proudly while we were hanging out, having a few beers. Well, he's fiddling and fiddling with the combination, and we realize if it takes much longer, we're not going to be able to drive home. (Too many beers.)

"Speed it up, Noel. Didn't you write it down somewhere?" we asked him.

"Yeah," he told us. "But I put the piece of paper in the safe."

So that's the organizational genius we decided to put in charge of our business. It was embarrassing! Our dad was just shaking his head at us saying, "*Tsjonge, jonge, jonge.*" That's Dutch for "boy oh boy." As in: what have you guys gotten yourselves into?

Noel was convinced that he knew how to get our T-shirts and merchandise made just because his parents had worked in the garment district, which is about the dumbest thing I've ever heard aside from this: we let him! HA!

Years later, Noel admitted that in managing us he was in way over his head; he had no business doing the job we gave him. He died recently. Another one down. Rest in peace, Noel. You were a lousy manager, but you were a fun guy. See you on the other side.

See, we didn't have time to overthink every aspect of our lives. We didn't even have time to *think*. We went from the house in Pasadena where we grew up to touring the world with Black

Sabbath. Suddenly, we were on the road, getting bigger and bigger, exploding. In a matter of months our lives were completely transformed. We were ready for the big time musically, but in every other respect we had no idea what to expect or how to handle what was thrown at us. We were still green.

We had a homecoming show planned at the Long Beach Arena after we got back from Japan. To our amazement, it sold out almost immediately. *Guys, we just sold out Long Beach Arena in less than an hour—how can that be?!* Well, they had decided to reverse the usual ratio of audience to stage; that's how. Looking at the poster for that gig now, I notice they promise an "intimate amphitheater style" gig. (I also notice that tickets cost $7.50. Ah, the seventies.) In an early example of our high spirits and marketing genius, we immediately started bragging about how we would have the biggest backstage on earth! Negatives can become positives pretty quick if you keep an open mind and learn how to shift your perspective. We're not retreating, we're just advancing in another direction!

I guess another word for that is "bullshit." Which we were not above. Dave convinced us all to lie about our ages, said it made us seem even more impressive if we pretended we were a little younger. Maybe it worked, who knows. ("That still causes me problems to this day," Ed complained years later. "I should've known when Roth said, 'Let's say we're two years younger than we really are.' And I'd say, 'Why? I'm only *twenty-two.*'")

That summer we opened for the Rolling Stones. July 13, 1978, at the Superdome in New Orleans, the same place they later put all the people displaced by Hurricane Katrina. Huge audience. Massive. It was obviously an incredible moment for all of us. But nobody was a bigger Stones fan than my roadie

Gregg. (I never called him my roadie, by the way; I called him "my associate.") What Zeppelin was to us, the Rolling Stones were to Gregg. Night before the gig we're at the hotel, hanging out, drinking. Gregg and I were being clods, as usual, a milder version of the guys on *Jackass*. We were doing that thing where it looks like you're running into the wall but you stop short at the last minute. Only Gregg forgot to stop. Next day he wakes up, his face is completely swollen; he looks like meat.

We go to do our sound check. We'd just gotten back from Japan, and I had these drums I picked up over there, Octobans. When we get to the venue I see some little guy is bending down behind my new drums. I'm about to yell at him, but then he stands up and it's Mick Jagger.

He couldn't have been friendlier or more collegial. So, after we talk for a little while, I say, "Mr. Jagger, my associate Gregg is your number one fan, would you mind saying hello to him?" And of course he's a total gentleman about it, and we walk over to Gregg and I do the introductions. Well, both of Gregg's eyes are swollen shut and he's wearing dark glasses; he can't see a thing. He extends his hand out into the middle of nowhere. His idol is standing two feet in front of him and he doesn't get to see him, doesn't get to shake his hand. He missed the moment. Story of Gregg's life.

Stine and I went to see him in 2005 about six months before I got the call that Gregg had shot himself. I didn't see the warning signs that day. He gave me all of the Van Halen memorabilia he'd accumulated over the twenty-odd years he worked for the band. (We had to let him go after I got sober in '87; I couldn't have someone around me all the time doing shots and pounding Schlitz, and Gregg wasn't willing or able to stop.) He handed over a tremendous pile of posters, T-shirts, Polaroids, and backstage passes from the seventies and eighties that day, and we had a good time looking through them together. Talking about everything we'd seen and done.

I didn't think anything of it. But in retrospect, of course he was settling his affairs, preparing for his big exit.

That's another guy I miss. See you on the other side, Gregg.

VAN HALEN WENT PLATINUM THAT OCTOBER, while we were in Germany with Sabbath. The record stayed on the charts for over three years. *Rolling Stone* put it on their list of the one hundred greatest debut records in rock 'n' roll history. We surpassed ten million copies in 1996. And I *still* hear those tunes on the radio when I'm driving my car.

In the end, that's all there is. You can't take fame or money with you when you check out. The greatest privilege in life is getting to create something bigger than yourself—something that has a life of its own, independent of you. All Ed and I can hope to leave behind are our children and our music. Our sons and our songs.

TEN

The disadvantage of being a rock star is your private life
is gone, but your sex life increases. And you have to do
interviews. I hate doing interviews.

—*Edward Van Halen, in . . . an interview*

When we got back to Pasadena, kids would follow us around and
chase us for autographs. There was a time when Ed and I looked
at each other and one of us—I can't remember if it was him or
me—said to the other, "Now I know what Elvis must have felt
like." That's an exaggeration, obviously, but that's what it seemed
like to us compared to our life before the tour.

Suddenly, you couldn't go to a movie, you couldn't go to a store,
you couldn't go anywhere. It was a very foreign experience, very
strange and unnerving. People you've never met before chasing
you down the street because they want you to sign a piece of
paper? That's some weird shit.

People react to fame in all kinds of ways. Some kids idolized us
back home, some kids resented us and thought we didn't deserve

what we'd gotten. "There's a lot of people who don't know me who hate me, because they think I'm some egoed-out motherfucker, but I'm not," Ed insisted. "That's just one thing I never expected." It really bummed him out. Like I told you: *sensitive.*

It took our parents some time to really register what was going on—to understand everything had changed. My mother was as focused on respectability and intellectual achievement as ever, so as you can imagine, there were aspects of our reputation that didn't thrill her. She was still telling us, "Wear a suit," and even, "Get a job!" (It's ironic that all the men in her life were in the only profession where you can get rich and famous without ever owning a suit, let alone wearing one.) Our father was proud, obviously, and he was pleased that we'd become what he'd always expected us to be: musicians.

But he understood how fleeting success and fame can be. One minute your songs are blasting out of every car in California, the next you could be back at the factory, churning out widgets for a living. He was aware that all of it could disappear overnight—and just because it *didn't* doesn't mean it *couldn't* have.

Dave had been waiting his whole life to be famous. He once told me, "I'm on from the moment I wake up." That's what he was like. He *needs* attention like everyone else needs water: to live. He always thought it was his destiny to be famous, and I guess he was right. Noel wrote that Dave "had always been, as they say, a legend in his own mind, and when legitimate stardom and success came his way, he devoured it like a drug."

He actually *liked* giving interviews to the press, something Ed and I dreaded and avoided at all costs. Talking about music is like dancing about architecture: we're players, not talkers. As Ed once said in—you guessed it—an interview, "Everything I've got to say is in the notes. It really is. I project more feeling out of playing than I can with my mouth."

But Dave *loved* to talk—about himself, about Van Halen, about martial arts and marijuana, philosophy and fornication, bagpipes and tailpipes. ("I've even started some of the interviews by saying, 'I'm glad you came here, I've got a few things I want to talk about,'" said Dave.) He just likes the sound of his own voice. Hell, I liked it, too, a lot of the time. "I think the two most difficult things to deal with in life are failure and success." Classic Dave line: kind of funny, kind of smart, and kind of bullshit. (My brother dying has been a lot more difficult than either.) "The reason the critics all hate Van Halen and like Elvis Costello so much is that they all look like Elvis Costello." Is there some truth to that? Of course! But why Dave found it necessary to offend the very people who were going to write about our band I'll never know. (Also, if you want to knock the critics, you're never going to top Frank Zappa. "Definition of rock journalism: People who can't write, doing interviews with people who can't think, in order to prepare articles for people who can't read." I guess he's dissing us, too, but from Zappa, I'll take it. Anyway, back to Dave . . .) "I'm not conceited. Conceit is a fault and I have no faults." Dave understood that being shameless, provocative, outrageous, and sometimes even obnoxious is all part of the game of showmanship.

Trying to get a rise out of people, doing and saying crazy stuff, it goes a long way. You go see the Chili Peppers jumping around naked, painted silver . . . you can't help but get into it. It's fun! It's weird! It's ridiculous! And it gives you permission to abandon the restraints of society. That's the spirit of rock 'n' roll, that defiance. It's about letting the whole human animal out of its cage. And of course—like every kind of performance—behaving that way is about getting attention. Ask Kanye. Ask Elon Musk! Now even the politicians follow that formula, acting out, saying the craziest things they can come up with, just to suck up a little more of the country's energy.

Ed and I wanted to play music for the rest of our lives—and not to have to do anything else to subsidize it. "To tell you the truth, I'm not into the star bullshit at all," Ed said, and he wasn't lying. "I don't even consider myself a rock star. I enjoy playing guitar. Period."

Fame was just something that came with that package. When we'd conceptualized it from a distance, we didn't really understand what it entailed. "What I dreamt was that we'd be famous," Ed once said, "but not that I'd walk down the street and everyone would go, 'Hey, that's him!' Not like that. Famous in the way that people *like the music we make*. I would love to be the invisible man: just play."

For Dave it was entirely the opposite: fame was the point! He would have been happy being a director or a movie star, whatever, as long as people were fussing over Diamond Dave. He got the idea to be a musician from us! "We went down to a place that they were playing. They were like fifteen or sixteen; that's how early Eddie and Alex were playing. It was just a small place but it was jammed," a friend of Dave's said in a documentary about our early years. "I think that was actually before Dave decided he really wanted to be a rock star, when we went and saw that, saw all that energy and stuff in that room." The adulation, the attention, the energy: *that's* what sucked him in. As my brother famously told *Rolling Stone*, "I'm a musician. Dave's a rock star."

But in the band, we needed both. Being thirsty for attention is not a bad thing in a front man. I think Noel Monk meant to be derogatory when he wrote, "Increasingly, I would notice David posing at every opportunity. Not just in the dressing room before going onstage but every time he passed a mirror or window. I would catch him pausing and vamping. Tossing his hair and sucking in his cheeks like a model." Sure, I know what he's talking about. If you spend any time around Dave and you have eyes in your face, you notice the guy preening. But that's part of his job! Visuals are the first way into a person's brain. Dave's vanity and his fascination with himself didn't bother me at that point. As far as I was concerned, it amounted to a kind of professionalism.

Look, Ed and I fought with him constantly. We fought with each other *about him* constantly. But at that point, we were still very much a team. "There was always that taunting and competing and chasing each other, and then running back up our tree and saying: 'I never heard you play better,'" Dave wrote. "Or cracking a joke and going, 'Hey, kid, what'd melody ever do to you?' This was mutual and it was furious and it was constant. There was conflict from day one."

He added, "It was healthy. To me it was the equivalent of smacking each other on our helmets before the kickoff in the football game. It's a version of support. It's how you show love."

PRETTY MUCH IMMEDIATELY AFTER OUR TOUR, the record people told us to get back into the studio. Can't we take a break? Have a little vacation? Nope. "We basically had three weeks left that year to finish our second record," Ed said. "We cranked out *Van Halen II* because that was what I had written." The record was composed of the songs we'd recorded for our demo that hadn't made the cut for the first album. Fortunately, there was still plenty of good stuff.

It wasn't just that we owed Warner Bros. a record, though. *You owe us a million dollars*, we were told—money they'd advanced us for our tour that somehow, mysteriously, all our record sales hadn't repaid. This was pretty startling. We'd sold two million records! I asked Ted Templeman, had we sold twenty million records, would we now owe you ten million bucks? How exactly does this formula work?

Our first record went gold, then platinum. We'd been working our asses off. And *we* owe *you* money?

As we soon learned, the band pays for *everything*. Staging, lights, road crew, venues, lawyers, managers, hotels, catering, bar tabs, you name it. The more money you make, the more money you owe. And if your record deal is terrible and you're only earning a pittance on each album, there's not a lot left over. This is when we started losing our innocence, you see.

Money is one of many reasons we kept living at home with our folks in Pasadena for years. "Living" isn't really the right word: we lived on the road. We couldn't really afford our own homes at that point, but then again, we wouldn't really have had any use for them. The month or two or three when we weren't touring, we were in the studio twenty hours a day making the next album—which we'd then go out on the road with as soon as it was humanly possible. There were times when I felt like a vampire who never saw the light of day. There's an old joke about what people in the music business think of the artists: you treat them like mushrooms—keep 'em in the dark and feed them shit.

One of the advantages of living with our folks was that you could hear everything going on in the house, so I was always aware of

what Ed was working on musically. I'd yell out encouragement—
"Yeah! That's a good one! Do that!"—because when you're creating
something new, sometimes you have no idea if it's any good and
it's helpful to have someone boosting your confidence, telling you
you're not wasting time. You're getting somewhere! "Alex and I
and my mom and dad, we're a very close family; I almost play to
please them," Ed once told an interviewer. "To get their seal of
approval: 'Yeah! I like that!' That means more to me than twenty
thousand people in an arena cheering."

It was obvious that our dad was lonely now that we weren't
around. We tried to pal around with him as much as we could
when we weren't in the studio. "We're going to retire him and
buy him a boat so he can go fishing," Ed told Steve Rosen at the
time (they recorded an interview in early 1979, just after we'd
finished our first tour—you can hear it on YouTube and listen to
Ed noodling on his unplugged guitar, giving Steve a preview of
the songs on *Van Halen II*). It seemed like the perfect way to pass
the time: out on the water with a beer, watching the clouds roll
by. We ended up with a wooden boat that could have collapsed at
any given moment, but man, did we love that thing. We named it
the *PT109*: when we were kids, there was a movie by that name
about John F. Kennedy's time in the service before he was president,
while he was the commander of patrol torpedo boat 109. We would
pile in with our buddies and our dad and a forty-horsepower
Evinrude engine and go out fishing for hours on end over in
Redondo or out on Castaic Lake, just hanging out with the guys,
and—unfortunately for me—waterskiing.

Gregg would drive the boat and whip me around like a maniac.
I loved it, I thought it was a blast, until one afternoon we were
going about sixty miles an hour and I fell. Hit the water with

such an impact it felt like smacking into concrete. We'd all been drinking for hours, and Gregg and our other friend who was there didn't even notice I'd gone down.

When I woke up, I was facing the sky. Fortunately, the life jacket had done its job and gotten my head above water before I blacked out. Eventually the guys realized what had happened and pulled me onto the boat. I didn't know it at the time, but I'd broken my neck. It healed wrong and caused me pain for years—I ended up collapsing before the tour in '95. But back in '79 when it happened? I was still immortal as far as I was concerned. That's the thing about being young: you think nothing can get you down, and most of the time, you're right.

THERE WAS A HURRY MAKING *Van Halen II* at Sunset Sound; we recorded ten songs in four days and we had a good time doing it. We never wanted to do more than three or four takes anyway, because then you start to lose the vibe and it feels artificial. The recording process was new enough to have the excitement of anything you're learning to do, where you're still figuring out the kinks. But we were also in the same room where we'd recorded our debut record, so we had more familiarity and comfort than we had the first time around; we felt more at home—both with the space and with Donn Landee and Ted Templeman, our collaborators at Warner Bros.

Like I said, we still had some of our old original music to work with: we'd recorded a version of "Beautiful Girls" on our demo (originally it was "Bring on the Girls," but we were getting classier. HA!). We came up with the tune "Outta Love Again" before Mikey was even in the band. One of my favorite moments on that album is the "guitar solo" in that song—which, if you listen to it, is very much a duet, a rock 'n' roll duet, for an electric guitar and drums. "You have to find your own voice," my dad always said about being a musician. Each of us had one, but then we had another one, together. I'm not trying to brag when I say that I'd be very surprised if anyone else could replicate our sound, our voice as brothers. I'm not saying we're the best, or even that we're better than anyone else! I'm saying we're us; we sound like *us* in the duet on "Outta Love Again." My contribution is a beat that's almost like jazz, but it swings *and* it's rocking. I'm happier with what Donn did here than I am with anything on our first album because I'm all over the kit and you can hear everything: he's got the mics on in such a way that it sounds like a real drum kit; you can hear the shells ringing. And Ed? All I can say is he sounds like my brother. Our sound together was an expression, an extension, really, of our relationship.

Some songs just kind of happen in the studio. That was the case with "Dance the Night Away"—never one of my favorites, too pop to qualify as *real* Van Halen as far as I'm concerned, but a huge hit for us nonetheless, and, more important, girls liked it. ("Light Up the Sky" was much closer to my idea of what we ought to be doing sonically.) Dave came up with the lyrics on the spot based on a true story: we once witnessed a drunk girl in the parking lot of Walter Mitty's having a quickie with her boyfriend. When they were finished and we were doing our set, we could see her in the front row, dancing for hours, just as happy as she could be—with her pants on backward! "A live wire, barely a beginner, but just watch that lady go. / She's on fire, 'cause dancin' gets her higher than anything else she knows." That was her, all right. Dave originally had the chorus as "Dance, Lolita, dance." Ed was the one who said, hmmm, maybe we're better off with "dance the night away." Good call.

They did the photo shoot for the album before we actually recorded it, and if you look at that crazy picture of Dave on the back cover—his legs flying out to the sides as he hovers in midair in those red-and-white-striped pants, his hand still clutching the mic stand even as he's airborne—you're seeing the moment just before Dave hit the ground hard in his Capezios and broke his foot. Consequently, he was on crutches when we recorded "Somebody Get Me a Doctor," and there was something hilarious about listening to him howl that tune, leaning into the mic, propped up on a crutch. "His injury just added to the vibe," as Ted put it. On the inside sleeve of the album we put a picture of Dave and his cane and his bandaged foot, chatting up some nurses.

Ted was much happier with Dave's singing now that we'd proven audiences wouldn't have a problem with it. "The reverb on Dave's voice is really good. I think we used the echo chamber at Sunset Sound for his vocals," Ted wrote. "It made Dave sound lonely, like he was yelling for help." You'll remember that less than a year earlier, Ted hated Dave's vocals so much he wanted him out of the band. So this was a significant improvement.

More important, *we* were more satisfied with the sound of the album after it was mixed and finished. "This album to me sounds heavier than the first, the overall sound is so much fuller," Ed told Steve Rosen when they talked shortly after the recording sessions. That was always what we wanted, and this time Donn and Ted had a better sense of what that meant to us. "I'm real happy with this record because it still sounds like Van Halen—which is three instruments and voices with very few overdubs, very live-sounding," Ed went on. Sounding on the record the way we sounded live was a point of pride for us. Ed never wanted to overdub something on a record he'd be unable to replicate onstage; I think it felt like cheating. Also, he didn't like to be separated from the rest of us: "It's just not the same as playing with the guys; there's no feeling there for me to work off of. I gotta feed off them to be able to play good."

Ted and Dave actually ended up being aligned a lot on this record. They got it in their heads we should record "You're No Good"—the Betty Everett song that Linda Ronstadt had already covered and had a big hit with in 1975. Never made any sense to me for Van Halen. "If it's been a hit once, you're halfway there"— that was Ted's logic. But I wasn't happy to have a cover as the first single on our second album. That song on that album still irks me.

Ted had just had a number one hit with another one of his artists, Nicolette Larson (who would later do some backup vocals for us), covering the Neil Young tune "Lotta Love." We recorded our own version of that one, too, as a joke. We kept the disco but changed the lyrics: "It's gonna take a lotta drugs, to get much higher than we are / It's gonna take a lotta drugs / Where's that fucking bar?" You get the idea. (The best was our substitution for "My heart needs protection / And so do I-ay-ay-ay-ay." It became "My nose needs perfection / Not Emerald Dry-ay-ay-ay-ay." Emerald Dry was this white wine Ted was always drinking.) When I listen to that recording it still makes me laugh, and it reminds me that Ted did have a sense of humor.

He lived in Pasadena, too, and he had us over to his house on New Year's Eve, when 1978 became 1979. Typical mansion, immaculate, looked kind of like a lawyer's office with all the leather furniture and those green lamps hanging over the desk. Ed picked up the Ramírez acoustic guitar that Ted had bought on a trip to Europe in the early sixties. "We sat on the couch in the living room and I watched him play these two-handed licks on it," Ted recalled. "I couldn't believe how powerful his playing sounded with no amplification. It was as jaw-dropping as when I heard 'Eruption' on the electric. What he played that night wasn't exactly 'Spanish Fly,' but he played all of these wonderful runs and chord patterns on acoustic that sounded like a complete left turn from what he'd done on 'Eruption.'" Ed was never going to be happy doing the same thing over and over. He wanted to grow! "That night just reinforced my belief in Ed's musical brilliance," Ted continued. "There were things I would have thought, before I met Ed, that a guitarist would not have been able to do on an acoustic. Ed's a true musical genius. He could pick up any instrument and play it. Once he picked up a reed instrument in the studio, it might have been a bassoon . . . I thought, *Man, he's not even playing a stringed instrument, and he's making music and it sounds good.* Regardless of the instrument, he almost intuitively knew what to do with it."

IN A WAY, THE TOUR for our second record was our first real tour because it was the first time we were headlining. That's a totally different animal. When you're the opening act you don't really have to worry about anything; you just show up and play. But ultimately you have to take off the training wheels and play for *your* audiences. Besides, as Marshall Berle once said, "Eventually no band wanted Van Halen to open for them, because they couldn't follow Van Halen!"

We called it the World Vacation Tour—which was kind of ironic because we hadn't had anything resembling a vacation in a long time. When you're headlining, you have to think about every detail: it's *your* tour, after all, who else is going to care? You want to create some excitement. We brought thirty-six *tons* of sound and lighting and staging wherever we went—and another ton of striped spandex pants and leather jumpsuits and God knows what else.

We got ourselves a better bus—we started out calling it the Defiance, and then somehow it became the Disco Submarine, despite the fact that we stayed above sea level, at least as far as I can remember. We did keep a six-man inflatable raft in the back of the bus in case the Disco Submarine ever started to sink . . . this was Dave's idea of being an urban guerilla. Another Dave idea: he hired a couple of what I believe we're now calling little people to serve as his security guards.

We specifically picked venues that we could sell out. People want what they can't have, it's just human nature: *Oh, man, I can't get into the Van Halen show? I have to see this band!* But that's not even the main reason we chose those locations. We want to make sure the rooms are full to capacity so that when everybody gets together and jumps around and yells, it's like the building expands! We want it so loud and sweaty and intense it's like a religious experience, and everybody there is participating in it. We're all in a communal sweatbox together creating an explosion! That's the idea of a Van Halen show.

When everything is firing on all cylinders and the band is smoking and the crowd is going crazy, there's nothing like it. Nothing on earth. "The main reason we didn't burn out on the road, even though we've been out for so fucking long, is that we really enjoy playing—it's not work," Ed told Rosen. "The work part is traveling, even that at times wasn't so bad . . . we walk onstage and even if I'm *dead* I still get off on playing." We loved to make music and we enjoyed creating the vibe, the party, for our audience. You realize people don't just come for the songs, they come to have an experience. And we loved being able to create that almost as much as we loved making music—occasionally, even more. It's a very thrilling thing to get a large group of people to unify and celebrate and go crazy. Makes you really feel *alive*.

"The only band with which I traveled that compared to Van Halen in the late 1970s and early 1980s was the Rolling Stones. And I don't think even they were as dynamic," Noel wrote. "I'm not saying Van Halen was a 'better' band than the Stones. I'm talking about the power of a live performance, the ability to captivate an audience. Van Halen was the best I've ever seen."

There's no substitute for being there, with us, in the moment. That's why we rarely did MTV Live or any of that—how can you compact all that energy onto a screen? The beauty of live music is the immediacy: once the song is done, that's it, forever. Every time we play, it's a little different; each song is whatever it is that night, that one time, right here, right now. (Hmm, good title for a song . . .) It's not the same thing as listening to a record.

Fortunately, a record was the next best thing, and the fans were buying them. *Van Halen II* was certified gold within a month of its release; it went platinum a month after that. And whereas the first record had peaked at nineteen on the *Billboard* chart, now we were number six.

EVERY TOUR HAS ITS TROUBLES. I started smoking again, unfortunately. It happened right after I went to the doctor with a bad heat rash I assumed I'd gotten from wearing sweaty stage clothes all the time. The doctor took one look at me and said, "Hey: your heat rash is *moving*." As in: you've got crabs, idiot. So then I'm sitting in my hotel room, nothing to do, miserable, crawling with crabs. I went down to Ed's room and said, "For God's sake, give me a cigarette."

I was promiscuous at that time in my life, because I was young and virile and I could be. Look, it's understood: guys in a rock bands get a lot of women; that's half the reason you do it in the first place! Recently someone sent me a meme, a picture of this sweet-looking kid behind a drum kit wearing a life preserver. Why the life jacket? Because he's a drummer: pretty soon he'll be drowning in it.

Ed and I would chase girls, or maybe they would chase us, but either way, that's not something you want your mother around for, so this became a problem when our parents came to see us on tour. She was always telling us, "You could do better!" And you know what? In this case, she was right.

Having sex with a lot of different people, a series of strangers, is theoretically about adventure and the thrill of the new. But it becomes a routine, like anything else: you play, you party, you flirt, you go upstairs. It became very one-dimensional, like telling the same joke every night to a different audience. Ultimately, I was lucky to meet someone I have what I can only describe as a cosmic connection with—I literally owe my life to Stine, my wife of almost thirty years. But I wasn't that deep back then. I was just into having a good time, all the time. Apparently, when I was partying backstage after a gig one night on the *1984* tour, I said, "I wish I had more than one dick!" in front of a (female!) reporter from *Rolling Stone*.

I want to be clear about something, though. Everything that Ed and I did with women, we did in the spirit of *mutuality*. We weren't looking to exploit other people; that's not how we were raised. My former neighbor Rod Stewart says, "I made *love* to every woman I've ever been with," and I can relate to that! "If you listen closely to Van Halen's lyrics," Dave said once on *Good Morning America*, "you won't find one sexist lyric. You won't find one victimizing sort of thinking. You won't find that victimization tact of thought." That's the truth!

Dave once told Noel he wanted to get paternity insurance in case someone got pregnant—or said she was pregnant—after a postconcert encounter with him. It never actually went anywhere, but from a marketing perspective it was genius. All the press said was that David Lee Roth had tried to insure his dick.

He talks a good game, but did Dave ever *really* have a girlfriend? Not that I can remember. (Think about the lyrics he sang on his own: "I ain't got nobody / Nobody cares for me, nobody, nobody / I'm so sad and lonely . . .") He's the only guy in Van Halen who never got married or had kids. Why? I'll let him tell you: "I 'spect I have not wound up with a significant other 'cause I'm not happy with me. Always something new to prove," he wrote. "Always something new to challenge. Always a new treasure mountain to climb."

We started the tour playing for around a hundred thousand people at the Los Angeles Memorial Coliseum at a concert they billed as the CaliFFornia World Music Festival—don't ask me what the extra F was for. Cheech and Chong were the MCs, Cheap Trick and Ted Nugent were performing, and Aerosmith was going on after us, coheadlining. A few weeks before the show, we went and scoped out the venue, and we got it in our heads that we should park a yellow Volkswagen Beetle on this hill near the stage where the entire audience could see it, and then we'd have all these announcements made throughout the day that it was in the way, and could Aerosmith please move their car? Then, when it was time for us to come on, we'd roll out in a Sherman tank and crush the VW—and, of course, figuratively, Aerosmith. We rented an actual Sherman tank at some place in Hollywood. We even bought two VWs to practice on, and the results were satisfying: we crushed those VWs like the bug they were named for.

It would have been great. Only problem was that Aerosmith got wind of what we had in mind, and they planned to retaliate by showing footage of airplanes blowing up tanks when they came onstage after us, which obviously would have given them the last laugh. So much for our tank shtick. The good news is we still blew Aerosmith off the stage. (And the backstage. Dave brought an orangutan dressed up like him so we had an extra party animal.)

We played a homecoming show at the Los Angeles Forum that our parents came to. "Playing the Forum is like a dream come true; I've seen everyone play there. It was a hell of an event for me," Ed said. "I come home and the back door is smashed in and all the records are gone." When we returned to Las Lunas Street, we discovered we'd been robbed while we were performing; all our gold and platinum records had been taken.

Wasn't hard to find the culprit. My mom had given a cousin of ours some menial work to do around the house and I guess the real reason he was there wasn't to paint the house, it was to case the joint. He wasn't the sharpest kid. He thought it was real gold in the record and he tried to melt it down. It's sad when you can't trust your own family. (But it's sadder trying to melt a gold record! Idiot!!)

As soon as we had the money, we got our parents a new place. That was a really satisfying thing to be able to do. Ed bought his first Porsche (a 911E Targa), which was almost as momentous—the beginning of a lifelong love of those cars, for both of us. (I still drive one. Or two.) Dave got a black Mercedes that he defaced with a giant skull and crossbones painted on the hood.

Now that money was coming in, we also encouraged our father to retire, which seemed like a good idea at the time. "He's been working seven days a week ever since we came to this country," Ed told a journalist. "The weekly checks out of our corporation pay us a lot more than he's making, so Al and I said, 'Quit your job.'"

Well, we never should have done that. I don't think it was emasculating or anything like that—he literally *made* us, after all; our success really was his, too. He's the one who taught us how to play music and he's the one who taught us the value of hard work. He comes to a new country where he's heard there will be all kinds of opportunities to play, and when he can't find any he works as a janitor to make ends meet, works in a machine shop, whatever it takes. I think the current generation doesn't have enough appreciation for taking responsibility like that—they can't even be on time, for crying out loud. For us it was deeply ingrained: *You are the head of the family. You have to provide.* And that's what he did.

Maybe without that sense of purpose he felt lost. The more he was at home, the less my dad seemed to enjoy life. Unfortunately, we didn't understand any of that at the time, and our good intentions screwed things up. We took away his sense of purpose.

It was a mistake that Ed and I both came to deeply regret.

ELEVEN

The reason we relate so well is because we *are* the
audience.

What we're doing onstage is what we always wanted to
see being done onstage. The reason it goes over so well,
I mean, we've traveled the world . . . even if they don't
understand the lyrics, don't understand exactly what
Dave is saying between songs, they get the feeling. They
relate.

And I think it's because there's a little bit of Van Halen
in everybody—and we're just there to bring it out.
Tonight you're with us, and we'll bring it *all* out.

—*Alex Van Halen, 1980 World Invasion Tour, local radio interview, Fort
Wayne, Indiana*

When I think of some of the things my brother and I felt the most
passionate about, I realize I'm seventy. You have to remember,
there was no internet when we were doing this, there was no MTV.

It was not a world where everyone films their thoughts on their phones sitting at home on the couch and then beams it around the world on TikTok so another person sitting on his ass can give it a thumbs-up. It was a world where people left the house! It was a world where the only real way to connect with a big group of humans was to go out and directly encounter them, preferably in a large space with great acoustics and booming volume. We wanted to record live, sure, but what we really wanted was to *be* live, in the flesh, physically—and psychically—connecting with our audience, and I'm not talking about the girls who came backstage after the shows. (Who am I kidding? I am. But not *just* them.)

I know I start to sound a little new age when I talk about this, but I don't care because I really mean it: we're sharing a moment in time and space with thousands of people, sometimes hundreds of thousands of people, and it's our job to set them on fire, emotionally (and to set my drums on fire, literally), for that time. "When the people scream so hysterically for such a sustained period of time, they're screaming for themselves," as Dave told *Rolling Stone*. "Not for me. Not because Eddie is so great. But because they see themselves reflected in us." For those few hours we are taking over a huge pack of humans: we're blasting music into their ears, getting them dancing, dominating their emotional and physical lives, bringing them into our traveling reality, making them a part of it.

Like I've said, my brother was always chasing a sound he could hear in his mind. We'd talk about the "brown sound," which was just our shorthand for a kind of earthy heaviness that we were into—"a rich, toney sound," as Ed once put it. Think wood, not metal. It was there in Zeppelin, but we started using that term in reference to this one snare drum of mine that I'd specially tuned, and it grew from there. "I want my guitar to sound like Al's snare," Ed said. "Warm, big, and majestic." We liked the same type of resonance, the same kinds of sounds, and that part was easy to figure out. What took a while was learning how to make them. It takes a long time to sound like you.

Ed bought an old Wurlitzer electric keyboard from a pawnshop outside of Detroit while we were on our second tour, and by the time we got back he had this one riff that he was just pounding out, over and over. I started drumming, and we must have played that song for a hundred hours. "Al and I jammed on the basic riff from 'The Cradle Will Rock' for two straight weeks," Ed said. "We didn't really know what to do with it, but we were having fun because it just sounded so wicked." We played it nonstop. Our joke was "We're just waiting for the next chord." And then one day, eureka, it showed up. "Out of nowhere the chorus came to us and it was finished," Ed said.

That's really how it happens. You keep on playing and the next chord comes—and then the next one. Just don't stop. The song will reveal itself. Michelangelo supposedly said that "every block of stone has a statue inside it, and it is the task of the sculptor to discover it." I'm not saying Ed was Michelangelo, but that's the basic idea. It feels like the songs—or the statues, or paintings, or poems, I bet—are floating around in the cosmos and what you're doing isn't so much writing them as looking for them.

Ed played that Wurlitzer through a Marshall guitar amp on our third record, *Women and Children First*. Finally, we had an album with no covers; every song was Van Halen down to the bones. I loved some of those tunes. "Romeo Delight" was a real hard rock classic—it became the perfect new opener for our shows; it never failed to get people going. The jungle drum intro to "Everybody

Wants Some!!"—there's a real tribal feel to that rhythm. You can imagine someone's about to go through a rite of passage when you hear that beat, or trying to summon healing spirits or wake the dead. You can see men dancing around a fire. And then Dave's singing about sex: everybody wants some. No arguing with that. Another primal element of humankind, like rhythm.

But who knows what else he's saying: "I took a mobile light lookin' for a moonbeam / You stand in line you get lost in the jet stream." Don't think for a minute I can decode that for you. But it somehow captures a feeling or a concept or *something* I'm familiar with. Some essence. It resonates, on a level that has nothing to do with logic. Just like music. Dave had this strange mix of flashes of brilliance interspersed with genuine insanity. And frankly sometimes the second trait was as valuable as the first.

"I always wanted Dave in the vocal booth when the other three guys were laying down tracks," Ted wrote in his book, "not something that I always had my other acts do . . . it was like having the Big Bad Wolf cartoon character in full view, and in the headphones, of the other three guys, and that was especially true for 'Everybody Wants Some.'" Dave was provocative, something to push against, and that's not a bad thing when you're trying to make something original. A certain kind of human friction can generate the energy necessary to create something. No friction, no heat. No heat . . . no fire.

We actually finished that record in Paris. Ted had to be over there for some reason, and he summoned us to join him—flew us over on the Concorde, the fastest passenger plane in the world at the time. (Dave and I wanted to record the sound of that roaring engine to use on our album, but it never quite came to pass.) I don't remember much about the recording sessions, we were so jet-lagged and loopy, but our nights out on the town were great, unforgettable, roaming the city passing around a bottle of champagne, checking out the discotheques and the clubs, and of course, the female Parisians. We could walk around there as free as a pack of teenagers in Pasadena. Nobody recognized us in France.

WE ALREADY KNEW HOW TO do the leather jacket, blue jeans, hard-drinking, tough-guy-who's-into-knives thing. We grew up around a version of that. So we welcomed the different outlook that Dave had in terms of aesthetics—a little bit more feminine, a lot more glitter. The Stones were actually the role model for that; they blurred the line between what's acceptable and what is not for a rock guy in terms of allowing androgyny to seep in. (It's partly because they're English. The English have some kind of pact that every man will dress up as a woman at some point in his life.) And then of course Freddie Mercury took it to the next level. So we were trying out all different things to see what would stick, and we were willing to give Dave some leeway on the visuals. When I look back at the photos from our recording sessions for *Women and Children First*, I can't help but notice Ed is wearing a pink jumpsuit. That's got to be Dave's influence—it certainly wasn't mine. The music was exuberant; we figured, why shouldn't we look that way, too?

Dave wanted Helmut Newton to photograph us for our third album cover. Newton was, to say the least, a legend. The guy was a once-in-a-generation talent who could make art out of whatever he was shooting. So we were into it.

But it got weird, fast. He had this idea—no doubt an idea that was influenced by Dave—that we should all be chained to a fence.

We didn't love that: We're Van Halen! *We* do the chaining. We had a hit song on the next album called "Unchained." (Coincidence? There are no coincidences.) It just didn't feel authentic to who we really were as a band. But it felt great to Dave. He was into a kind of homoerotic S & M thing. I don't mean sexually, but aesthetically he was up for whatever he thought would get him the most attention. Life was a costume party for him—it's not like a look ever reflected some deeper commitment to a way of life for Dave. He bought this old '49 Mercury lowrider, for instance. We opened the trunk and there were bags of *concrete* he had put in to make it lower! For God's sake, get some hydraulics, do it properly! We loved cars and we thought that was sacrilege. The point is that none of these aesthetic choices of his reflected a real depth of experience.

But let's get back to the story. We did the shoot at Dave's dad's house in Pasadena—it was a beautiful property, lots of palm trees and this grand stone staircase leading up to the house, which was a ten-bedroom Mediterranean mansion that was so important the city actually paid to have it renovated to its original condition. (Eventually, Dr. Roth handed the house down to Dave, and he lives there to this day.) The problem, though, is that gave Dave the upper hand, and at a certain point in the shoot he said we needed more chains and he sent us off to get them. Well, we never liked photo sessions anyway, so off we went to the local hardware store.

I realize now that Newton was only really interested in shooting Dave, and this was his chance. I think they'd planned the whole thing in advance, and that was insulting—I wish they'd just told us what they wanted (not like we would have said yes). Here's the thing: Dave was always great at making the sale. And then 90 percent of the time he had a great rap but couldn't actually deliver. When it came down to *doing* it, it just didn't quite work. This was no exception.

He got the pictures he wanted. But we were never going to okay an album cover that didn't feel like Van Halen. This is our band. This is our brand. This is what we've worked for our whole lives! And neither the two guys actually named Van Halen nor our record company was ever going to do what Dave *really* wanted, which was to have just *him* on the cover, as if he were the star and we were just there to back him. (An idea Ed and I thought was hilarious. We grew up on music that didn't even *have* lyrics: the players were the important part; the words and the singer were just the icing on the cake. The music itself is what elicited emotion. Dave's counter to that was always, "Nobody leaves the concert humming the guitar solo.")

Of course, Warner Bros. was already however many thousands of dollars in with this Newton thing, and they didn't want that to be a complete waste. So even though we felt like it was contrary to the band's interest to picture only one of us—especially one of us in chains—and even though the Newton picture didn't feel like Van Halen, we had to include his portrait of Dave as a yard-long poster in the first million copies of the album. Fans got a kick out of it. But the whole thing left a bad taste in my mouth. Dave was already starting to try to steer the band into a zone that just wasn't who we were. We were at cross-purposes.

Once the visual starts to intercede too much, it's no good—especially when you've got a talent like Ed's. I had this discussion with Donn Landee just the other day, and his response was that with a talent like Ed's, no visual could ever overpower it. Sure, that's true. But it's like when you watch the movie before you read the book. Now that movie is imprinted on your brain! You don't get to draw your own conclusions, invent your own pictures, when you read the book after you've already seen the movie. And Ed and I were very aware of that. The music was the point. We never wanted to invest more energy in our image than we did in our playing, and there is only a finite amount of time in the day. We are either touring or making an album basically *all* of the time, Dave; let's not spend too much of the brief window in between focusing on the visuals.

I told you: I'm seventy. Ed and I were dinosaurs. We were born at the right time for our talents and passions, an analog reality where Zeppelin was king, without ever shooting a single video. If you saw them in pictures, you saw *all four* of them. And none of them were tied to a fence.

OUR RECORD WENT GOLD WITHIN a week of its release. "The haste with which *Women and Children First* bullied its way into the top ten suggests that there's a little Van Halen in everybody," read the *Rolling Stone* review (borrowing my line!). Formally, we called our third tour the World Invasion. The Party Till You Die Tour is what we called it off the record. As all our backstage passes warned, WDFA—We Don't Fuck Around.

Everything we did, we did to the maximum. Why have a glass when you could drink the whole bottle? Ed and I had been taught: no mediocrity. Even when we failed, we failed *spectacularly*. (I'm looking at you, *Van Halen III*.) If we made a mess, it was a big effing mess.

We set off for a third time in early 1980. We get to Pueblo, Colorado, to play the University of Southern Colorado four days after the album comes out. They've never had a massive rock concert there before, and they have no idea how to handle one, as it soon becomes clear. We, on the other hand, took professionalism seriously. Our riders were very specific and carefully constructed, and a lot of this was for safety: If you don't have the right wiring for our electrics, there could be a catastrophic fire. You don't have enough support to hold up all of our equipment? The floor could cave in. (Stay tuned.) And so, just to make sure the promoters and the venues were reading all the fine print and paying attention to our requirements, we tucked a weird little demand in there that you've probably heard about at some point: no brown M&M's. We wanted that candy backstage, but, underlined, in all capital letters, we made it perfectly clear: "M&M's (WARNING: ABSOLUTELY NO BROWN ONES)."

I know. We sound like jerks. Like rock star prima donnas looking to make some poor kid sit around picking through candies till he goes blind. But it wasn't about a power trip, and it wasn't about some strange aversion to the color brown—think about it: our tone of choice was the brown sound. (When interviewers would ask Ed and me if the brown ones tasted different from other M&M's, we went with it, though, played it up for yuks: "Yes, they do. They are more heavily sugarcoated, they contain more chocolate," I replied very seriously on one radio show in Indianapolis as Ed started cracking up next to me. "The green ones and the yellow ones are much more refreshing.") Really, it was about devising an easy-to-spot indication of a venue's attention to detail. If we see brown M&M's, we know: we are not in the hands of professionals. If they didn't bother with this, what else didn't they bother with, what other corners are being cut? So now we can't relax. Now we have to worry about something other than just making great music. And we're going to express our displeasure about it.

The first logical step after we saw said M&M's backstage in Pueblo was to grind them into the carpet. And then it kind of went from there. Little by little the whole buffet became fair game, and before you knew it, we were chucking drinks at each other, and flinging mashed potatoes against the wall, and hurling fried chicken across the table. One of the campus officials told the local paper that we behaved "like a bunch of animals," saying, "They ate lasagna with their hands, threw the food around the room, smeared the food on the walls and on each other. In one of the men's rooms nearby . . . it's unmentionable what happened there." It may be unmentionable, but it wasn't our doing. Five thousand people came to our show, and I guess our performance inspired an appetite for destruction in the students, too, because they're the ones who trashed that bathroom. We were busy having a food fight that rivaled the one in the movie *Animal House*, both in vigor and, eventually, in notoriety. The university decided they wouldn't be hosting any more rock concerts.

But honestly? They were the real degenerates, not us. They had just put in some kind of shock-absorbent floor that couldn't handle the weight of our equipment and staging, and guess what? We had a cave-in that caused ten or twenty thousand dollars' worth of damage to our lighting trusses and other gear. We're lucky nobody got injured—or killed! The brown M&M's really *were* an indication of a host that didn't pay attention to the specifications of our contract, didn't take their responsibility for safety anywhere near seriously enough, and didn't understand or respect the time and money and energy that we put into crafting a stage show on the grandest possible scale.

Unfortunately, when you bring thousands and thousands of people together and assist them in releasing their inhibitions, not everything that happens is pretty. Guys would get in fights, get drunk, all the things that guys do. And sometimes there would be trouble that had nothing to do with that; local law enforcement was just looking for a reason to crack down on guys with long hair who liked rock 'n' roll. At our show in Cincinnati at the Riverfront Coliseum, 177 people got arrested, mostly for smoking weed in the parking lot, or violating the ban on open flame inside the coliseum when they lit their cigarettes or held their lighters up in the air the way kids used to do at concerts in the pre-vape era (a time when the average pair of jeans had a Bic in at least one pocket). The cops even charged Dave with "inciting the crowd" that night, because he howled, "Light 'em up" . . . which is one of the *lyrics* in our song "Light Up the Sky."

A good show costs a ton of dough. Looking through an old budget, the cost of rehearsal alone was a hundred thousand bucks, and that's over forty years ago . . . in today's dollars it would be closer to 400K. You've got to pay your crew for that time, you've got massive traveling costs ahead of you, you need security at this point, and then there's renting staging and lights. An "ego ramp" alone—that piece of staging that shoots out into the audience so Dave can dance his way into the crowd—cost us five grand a night then, so we're talking closer to 20K now. But it was worth it to us.

All of us were still putting our money right back into the band; we were nowhere near rich at this point, even though we'd sold millions of records. How is that possible? "We break even because we put all our money into sound and lighting," Ed—accurately—

told *Guitar Player* in 1980. "We always bet our all, give it all or nothing. We are not about to go, 'We can save a little money here if we don't do that.' We design what we want, have it built, and then say, 'How much money have we got?' If we don't have enough, we say, 'We've got to get it.'" We had everything worked out meticulously so that wherever we went, the show would look like the music sounded: bigger than life. We knew: the audience remembers how you made them *feel*. Every element of our show contributed to that and was a direct reflection of our band.

You want to give the audience what they paid for; that was something we took extremely seriously because to us it amounted to our integrity, our professionalism. Ironically, in our line of work, this meant engaging in behavior that would get you thrown out of pretty much any other place of business. The fans don't want to see a bunch of guys drinking green juice who look like they're on their way to the library. They want to see wild, un-inhibited, virile maniacs. You need to be doing everything they wish they could be doing. And we were pretty good at fulfilling those roles. It was our *job* to be animals.

Animals who somehow stayed in peak physical condition. And that's the tricky part. Because if the audience is living vicariously through what's happening on the stage, then what's happening better be superhuman. Whether you're jumping up into a split, sliding across the stage, flying down from the rafters on a wire, or, as I did on the next tour, pounding a massive flaming gong at the end of every show, whatever you do has to be huge, energetic, unforgettable. So you'd better be fit.

Because you have to do it the next night, again. And the night after that. And the one after that, too. And when you're not doing it, you've got to be traveling hundreds or thousands of miles, sleeping on planes or on the back of a tour bus, and then there's the all-important responsibility of pounding Schlitz Malt talls by the dozen and keeping our female fans entertained after the show. By the World Invasion Tour, we were all starting to hurt. But we knew that it was our job to keep pushing everything to the maximum regardless.

Like I told you, WDFA.

DAVE IN PARTICULAR WAS INTO feats of exertion at that point in his life. He started working out with the trainer for the LA Lakers. He went hiking in the Star Mountains of New Guinea with these guides who called themselves the Jungle Studs (which is either hilarious or pathetic depending on what kind of mood you're in). When we were in Italy promoting the record, Dave was doing his jumps off the drum riser for a photo shoot and he bashed his nose on a low-hanging disco ball. (Yes, I'm serious.) The European press got a big kick out of his bandaged-up nose, and he liked the publicity so much I think Dave broke his nose a second time spinning the mic stand years later, when we were performing on Jimmy Kimmel, just so he could get more attention! Dave *is* showbiz.

More European medical weirdness: for reasons that elude me now, our distributors in France had us shoot a promotional video for the song "Loss of Control" in an operating room. You have to give them credit: there was no MTV, no VH1, they weren't just rolling with the tide, they were ahead of it. You can look it up online and, man, that video is weird. It starts out with Dave lying on the stage screeching with a pretty nurse on top of him. But it doesn't look sexy or anything; it looks more like she happened to get shot with some kind of tranquilizer dart and fell on top of him, smiling strangely while he screams. Then he's up and dancing in a doctor's coat over his striped spandex and suspenders; the rest of us are playing in scrubs, and I've got X-ray film stuck on my drums.

Two things strike me about that video now: the first is that Dave shoves himself into every shot. The camera lands on me drumming? Dave gets behind my kit and vamps. They want to show Ed jamming in his scrubs? Dave's throwing himself in front of the guitar. He *had* to get in the shot; it was like his life depended on it. The second thing I notice: there are all these tight shots of the nurse with her face hidden behind a surgical mask. Now that we've all spent years trapped behind masks like that trying not to give or get the COVID virus, the whole thing takes on an eerie resonance.

I will hand it to the Europeans: they got the general idea of videos before there was such a thing as videos. You pick a theme that doesn't really make sense and hang on for dear life. (Why exactly are we being medical here? Why is Dave breaking into an air traffic control spiel but looking like he's about to perform surgery in the Rainbow Room? Nobody knows.) Videos were abstract things in those years before the form was really cemented. And back then every country had its own creative team affiliated with the label, so you were constantly finding yourself in some country where you didn't speak the language, thinking you were misunderstanding what they wanted you to do because it was just so outlandish: "Am I hearing this right? You want me to play drums under the neck of a life-sized brontosaurus?"

That's what I was thinking the following year when we found ourselves inexplicably playing "So This Is Love?" in a clearing in the middle of the woods outside Milan for Italian television, surrounded by giant dinosaur statues at the Rivolta d'Adda Prehistoric Park. It's an insane bit of footage, look it up. There's a woolly mammoth, a T. rex, and my brother wearing red-and-white-striped socks up to his knees and a matching T-shirt. (He wore that outfit into the ground.) Dave has some ridiculous scarf that looks like a piano keyboard looped around his neck with his hairy chest out, and he's humping his way up a dinosaur leg.

That was the prehistoric, if you will, era of music videos, when sound was still the point and images were secondary in the record business, before MTV threw the balance completely askew. Dave, of course, had no problem with this shift because he was always more interested in communicating with an audience through hair and dance and shoes than we were, and less interested in making innovative music. I don't even mean that to be disparaging! We were good at some things and he was good at others; same with Mikey.

Sitting with Dave in interviews was a trip—it was so clearly and flamboyantly an extension of his stage persona, his great creation, Diamond Dave. He was like a carnival barker. It was like he was following the rules of the stage—no dead air—at all times. As he once told me, "I'm on from the minute I get up." So he'd just be yakking, nonstop, and I'd be sitting next to him laughing because often, he was clearly making absolutely no sense to the interviewer, but I got it. Maybe because of his ADD, he would just buzz from one subject to the next like a fly trapped in a car, zipping all over the place. I knew the way his mind worked, so I could usually understand what he was getting at, but you could tell the journalist was baffled and wondering, *Is this guy for real?*

He loved to talk but it was rare that he *really* knew what he was talking about. He usually had a kind of remedial, buzzword-level understanding of whatever matter he was philosophizing on—the state of music, Pop Art, whatever—but I'm not sure he knew there was always more to it. Dave was a pseudointellectual, a dilettante, who knew a little about a lot of things but only knew a lot about one thing: himself!

His passion for publicity created a dilemma. On the one hand, *this is great*. We don't like talking, and because Dave can't get enough of it, we really never have to. (And there was a constant demand: once you start playing the fame game instead of just playing music, a kind of momentum picks up, and the next thing you know you're devoting all kinds of time and energy to feeding the machine. You want to be on the cover of the magazine? You got to do the interview; you got to spill your guts. No thanks, we're trying to run a band here, and that's a full-time job!) But the problem is that we can't always let Dave do it by himself. You can't have one person out there representing Van Halen, creating the impression that he *is* the band. When Peter Grant was managing Led Zeppelin he was always very clear when it came to publicity: you get them all, or you don't get any of them. That's the brand; that's the band. So there's the paradox.

You need to be an organism that holds *together*—in the eye of the public but also in reality! Because a band is a delicate balance. And that becomes evident in who gets which room and who gets which part of the bus and so on. People start to get weird about the pecking order. There's a lot of jockeying for territory, whether it's creative territory, or who gets to decide the order of the songs on the album, or who gets the first burger and who has to wait two minutes longer for his to come out. On tour, there are a million little opportunities a day to not get your way and to feel slighted. There are a million opportunities to be a dick and make an issue out of something that you ought to just let slide.

"Success has always been the greatest liar," Nietzsche wrote. Dave's hearing a sea of topless women screaming that they want him and throwing their lingerie at him every night, and guess what? He starts believing he's entitled to a certain kind of treatment, a certain kind of primacy. "As smooth and cordial as David could be in guiding the course of an interview, he was often exactly the opposite in dealing with technicians and support staff and even his bandmates," in Noel's opinion. "He was fussy and easily annoyed and had little use for diplomacy." Imagine saying, "Enough with the guitar solos"—to *Edward Van Halen*! It's not only rude, it's deranged!

But by the same token, Ed has every magazine, every musician, telling him he's the greatest guitarist who ever lived. And he says he's just a vessel, he sounds humble, but at some level that message—and plenty of coke—starts messing with his head. He's less willing to put up with Dave's insanity. He has less of a sense of humor about it when Ted pushes back on some far-out idea. "The work, whether of the artist or the philosopher, invents the man who has created it," Nietzsche continued, ". . . 'great men,' as they are venerated, are subsequent pieces of wretched minor fiction."

Or, to put it another way, you start to believe your own bullshit. You lose sight of the fact that you may be the soup du jour now, but in the context of the universe, you're still nothing but a speck.

TWELVE

Could this be magic? Or could this be love?

Could this turn tragic? You know that magic often

does.

And I see lonely ships upon the water,

Better save the women and children first.

Sail away with someone's daughter,

Better save the women and children first.

—*Van Halen, "Could This Be Magic?"*

It's an apt coincidence (I don't believe in coincidences) that the album we were promoting was *Women and Children First*, because during our swing through Louisiana, Ed met the woman who became the mother of his child.

Valerie Bertinelli heard our music for the first time when she borrowed our records from her brothers. She was already famous for playing Barbara Cooper on the Norman Lear sitcom *One Day at a Time*, but she was still only nineteen. And she was the breadwinner for her entire family. That's a lot of pressure and a lot of power for a teenager, which is what she was when the Bertinellis moved to Los Angeles so Valerie could pursue her television career. She showed up backstage at our show in Shreveport, her hometown, that summer, with a brother or two and a present for the band: a bag of M&M's. (A note to the wise: August is not the time to visit Louisiana. It was *sweltering*.)

They were a fun hang, those brothers—the Nellies, I called them. The first night we met them, Mikey and the Nellies did some serious drinking, which culminated in a fire-extinguisher fight. Valerie was *there* for Ed. "You had to peel me off the floor," is how she's described her immediate crush on my brother. (Our tour manager Steve Vando and I had this shtick at that time that you can tell if a woman is going to sleep with you within one minute of meeting her. If you're not getting anywhere after one minute, you move on to the next one. I think Ed knew within fifteen seconds.)

"It was kind of cute to see them together—they were both clearly nervous and somewhat reticent," Noel wrote about that night. "This struck me as a sign of genuine chemistry. After all, Valerie had spent most of her life in front of a camera or audience; she was completely comfortable with all manner of public interaction. And yet, here she was, stammering and blushing like a schoolgirl in the presence of the captain of the football team." Valerie came to our next show, too.

Almost immediately, Dave didn't like it—that there was this new celebrity energy around that had nothing to do with him. Here's how he describes their first meeting: "One of the front office guys comes in and he says, 'Dave, this is Valerie Bertinelli.' I had no idea who she was. Had no interest at all." You get the idea. He was just negative about her from the word "go." Remember:

fame was the whole point for him. And at that time Valerie had a huge audience—*everybody* knew who she was. So she was sucking up some of the attention in the Van Halen orbit and it drove Dave crazy.

How do I know? We're living on a *bus* together: you can almost hear each other think! And Dave would make little comments about how important it was for our image that we didn't have girlfriends, that we were young and untamed and had a lifestyle that fans could aspire to . . . they're living vicariously through us even when we're not onstage. Now, all of that is true. Rock 'n' roll is an extension of your enjoyment, of your perception, of life: everything has to be bigger; everything needs to be *more*. And Dave can be very persuasive. But Ed's my brother. If he wants to tie himself down—at the tender age of twenty-three!—and that's what he thinks is going to make him content, then so be it. "I don't like one-night stands," he told *Rolling Stone*. "I don't like getting the clap. I want to have kids. I want to go through life with somebody."

I figured he and Val looked so much alike, when they had the kid, even if it looked like her, it'd still look like him! HA!

All kidding aside, the two of them really got along.

I was happy for him.

HARD ROCK HAD BEEN OUT of fashion when we started out in the clubs; it was the era of the singer-songwriter. Look at the covers of *Rolling Stone* from the late seventies: Bruce Springsteen; Carly Simon; Linda Ronstadt; James Taylor; Jackson Browne. You take a blender; you throw in the antiwar movement, a pair of moccasins, a lot of long brown hair, an acoustic guitar, and a bunch of major seventh chords; and voilà, you've got yourself the easy-drinking milkshake that is the singer-songwriter. Blink your eyes and now the pendulum has swung completely the other way, from these soulful, harmless crooners to the plastic pop of the Go-Go's, the Cars, Devo—also a bunch of benign white people, but with skinny ties and synthesizers (not that there's *anything* wrong with synthesizers!!!). We, obviously, didn't fit in with any of this, or anything else that was happening at that time—not disco, not punk, not folk, not funk. I'm starting to sound like Dr. Seuss.

Van Halen's ascent was "both inspiring and confounding" to other bands, we learn in *Nöthin' but a Good Time*, an oral history of the "eighties hard rock explosion" by the music journalists Tom Beaujour and Richard Bienstock. According to those two, Van Halen's "electrifying live performances, striking blond-maned front man, and resident guitar wunderkind were such an undeniable force that they transcended the record industry's genre bias and landed a deal with Warner Bros. Records. The group's success, however, did not trickle down to other acts occupying the same stylistic lane." They quote Mick Brown, the drummer for the band the Boyz and later Dokken, saying, "No one seemed to be interested in the other bands, which I thought was weird, because it was like, 'Don't you think the record companies would want, like, nine more Van Halens?'"

The answer is pretty clear, isn't it? There *weren't* any more Van Halens. We were a genuine original.

"I guess they say that imitation is the highest form of flattery, but I think that's a crock of shit," my brother said. "What I don't like is when someone takes what I've done, and instead of innovating on what I came up with, they do my trip!" He was obviously happy to *inspire* others, but he didn't appreciate being knocked off.

Which even happened at *our own* gigs—twice! When we played a stadium with Boston in the summer of '79, their guitarist Tom Scholz incorporated a chunk of "Eruption" into his own solo. He probably thought it was a tribute, but we thought it was weird as hell. Believe it or not, the same thing happened on our tour in '78: the guitarist Rick Derringer opened for us in Texas, and he lifted the tapping sequence from "Eruption." Ed remembered, "After the show we're sitting in the bar, and I said, 'Hey, Rick, I grew up on your ass. How can you do this?'" And then Derringer did it *again* the next night, so we kicked him off our tour.

People copied Ed's guitars as well as his playing. Charvel—a manufacturer he had loved—started selling a copy of Ed's guitar: a Strat-style body with a humbucker and a tremolo. He had to sue them to get them to stop. Then a guy asked if he could use Ed's name to market a special pickup he wanted to manufacture. Ed said no way. "Next time I pick up *Guitar Player* magazine there's a special Van Halen model," Ed fumed. Eventually we got that stopped, too. But there was no stopping kids from copying Ed's stripes, painting them on their guitars—they were everywhere you looked. "Just the other night, Christmas Eve, I went to the Whisky. A band called the Weasels was playing, and the lead guitarist had a guitar exactly like mine," Ed said. "I just don't understand how someone can walk onstage with my guitar, because it's my trademark." Being an original himself, he just didn't understand why so many people are desperate to emulate somebody else.

As the eighties picked up speed, glam rock and heavy metal were heaving their way into the Top 40, invading the mainstream, and whether we liked their music or not, a lot of the bands that were hot in Hollywood had been influenced by Van Halen.

There were so many of them in the eighties, it was like a virus swept the Sunset Strip: Ratt, Mötley Crüe, Warrant, Guns N' Roses, Poison, Stryper, Whitesnake, White Lion, Great White, Road Crew, Twisted Sister, Cinderella . . . just making this list is giving me a headache. "All of a sudden you see these bands like Mötley Crüe and Poison and what's the common thread between all these bands? All their singers had bleached-out blond hair, they all wanted to be David Lee Roth," Michael said. Dave was firmly in the imitation-is-the-sincerest-form-of-flattery camp. He befriended Vince Neil and introduced Mötley Crüe when they played the Troubadour.

But those bands weren't up to our standards musically. For us, hair and makeup, crazy clothes, and a great show with things bursting into flames, that was all just the icing on the cake. For most of the eighties hair metal bands, that stuff was the entire piece of pastry. Well, as Dave used to say, Van Halen can play under nothing but a bare lightbulb and we'll still kick your ass.

OUR FOURTH ALBUM WAS TOUGHER and less buoyant than the ones that preceded it. It's harder rock, and maybe just a little bit of an FU—or at least a challenge—to our imitators. It was, as we titled it, a Fair Warning: It doesn't matter if you have long hair and leather pants and an androgynous blond front man. There's only one Van Halen.

The music on that record had some menace to it. "It's all over but the shouting, I come, I take what's mine," Dave sings on "Mean Street"—when Ed isn't *raging* on the guitar. That was very much the spirit of *Fair Warning*. Dog eat dog. "What made Van

Halen tick, more than anything else, was a primal approach to the social contract," as Dave once put it. "We're only at our best when we're ascending toward something. And when you're ascending, you're furious, you're focused; you have to be or you'll fall off." Furious and focused. That was us.

I found this image by a Canadian-Ukrainian artist, William Kurelek, that I wanted to use on the record jacket, a painting of a guy pushing against a brick wall with his head. Kurelek was like us: an immigrant who arrived in Canada without speaking a word of English who had to adapt. He was a cultural outsider with the benefit of a talent, in his case visual art. If the aftermath of the Second World War and its toll on our old man shaped our worldview, the brutality of World War I was Kurelek's reference point. His paintings were a response to that history—and to the savage side of human nature in general.

Well, that's the side we made music about, especially on *Fair Warning*. We were very much in touch with our inner barbarians. A regular feature of our creative process, our working environment, was a gladiatorial clashing of wills—and of bodies from time to time. Ed and I would get into arguments and the next thing you know we'd be on the floor wrestling, cursing at each other in Dutch, same as we had been since we were kids. "We fight more than anyone I've ever known but we also get along better than anyone I know," Ed said. "Alex and I, we're brothers: without him I don't know how I would handle all of this."

Kurelek's painting of that man, plowing his head against the wall, to me represented the sense of struggle that's part of being alive—and certainly part of being in a band. No matter how hard you fight for your point of view, when you're a member of a group, you're constantly making concessions, and frequently resenting them. Ed told an interviewer from *Creem* around that time, "I'm doing exactly what I want. People ask me if I want to cut a solo album, and I say 'What the fuck for?' Playing with Van Halen is like doing a solo album. Complete freedom to do what I want." Total BS! In a band, there's no such thing. You never stop making compromises, large and small. That's the price you pay for collaborating.

The painting I wanted is on the *Fair Warning* album cover, for instance, but it's just one of a patchwork of Kurelek images, most of them depicting some kind of violence or cruelty. (Much too busy!) So I sort of got what I wanted, but not really. Welcome to life in a band.

For the first time, Ed was doing heavy overdubs on the guitar tracks. And for the first time, our record was really created *in* the studio, as opposed to the previous records, which all had songs we'd written in Dave's basement and played for years in the clubs. Consequently, there was a lot of Ted in the process, too much for our taste. "During *Fair Warning* Ed came to me," Donn Landee told me recently. "I was mixing or putting something together, staying late, and Ed said, 'I want to be able to work with you alone; I don't want Ted to be around. I can't play in front of him.' I said, 'Sure you can! I've seen you play in front of twenty thousand people!' He said, 'That's different, that's easy. Playing for one guy who's going to have the *judgment* just freaks me out.' He told me, 'I can't play in front of Ted, and I can't play in front of the woman I'm going to marry. It's just too much pressure.'"

It all came to a head when we were recording "Unchained" (because Ed felt shackled, ironically). "Ted didn't like what Ed was playing and Ed did not want to play what Ted was suggesting," Donn recalled. "That whole day, making that whole song fit together, was crisis after crisis—there was no other day like that I had working with anybody, ever. Ted *tortured* Ed, and to this day he doesn't know it."

Ted realized Ed was never completely uninhibited when he was around. "There wasn't a better guitarist walking the earth in 1981 than Ed Van Halen, but I could tell that he'd sometimes get nervous around me when we were working in the studio," Ted wrote in his book. "When I was gone, he loosened up." But it was bigger than that. Ed was at odds with Ted because he felt like he knew more about music than any producer—which was the truth—and he wanted the freedom to try new things. To hear Ted tell it, he was doing his best to accommodate Ed: "Occasionally, when he was trying to push the envelope, I couldn't decode and translate what he was after," Ted continued. "I don't think Ed ever knew how frustrated I felt when he would try to articulate a sound or feeling to me and I couldn't dial it up for him. I always wanted to make him happy."

That's probably true. But it ain't the *whole* truth. Ted was at odds with Ed because he'd produced a lot of hit records—by everyone from the Doobie Brothers to Little Feat to Van Morrison—and it was his job to produce more of them. Ted was a company man. Ed's desire—his need, really—to keep growing creatively and to experiment with new styles and sounds was in conflict with Ted's agenda to reproduce the winning formula of the past.

This was an issue with Dave, too. We'd always come from opposite ends of the musical spectrum in terms of taste, but it was getting more difficult to find the overlap, the style that combined his flamboyant weirdness with our sound. Don't get me wrong, we still achieved it; *Fair Warning* is a great record if you ask me. Or Ted, for that matter: "There were lots of heavy metal bands that put monster riffs together with memorable lyrics. But none of them could match Van Halen's songcraft and humor. The breakdown of 'Unchained' underscores what helped separate Van Halen from their competitors." Even though we didn't have a big pop single to feed the machine, we still had our third platinum record in *Fair Warning*, and it went to number five on the *Billboard* chart, setting a new high for us.

Listen, we all loved the record. It was something different for us, not a party album. It's always satisfying to show another side of yourself as an artist, to surprise people a little and suggest that there's more to you than just what they've already seen. *Fair Warning* was darker and less exuberant and, in some ways, more musically interesting than our earliest records. But making it was an aggravating process. "On the whole album I was angry, frustrated," Ed has said. He wanted to do longer, stranger solos. He was into progressive rock, and this was the beginning of his fascination with the British jazz fusion guitarist Allan Holdsworth. (He even convinced Ted to give Holdsworth a record deal; Ed wanted to coproduce him. Whole thing fell apart before it ever got off the ground. It was arrogance on Ed's part to get involved.) Dave had genuinely different taste, but he also had a different agenda that had started to cause real tension: he wanted to be as famous as humanly possible. And he was convinced our musical instincts wouldn't lead him there. You remember his mantra: "Nobody leaves the concert humming the solo."

But there was another issue with Dave that was just as explosive: Valerie.

"My read was that Dave didn't like all the press attention that Ed (and Valerie) had garnered," Ted wrote. It was obvious to anyone who was in our immediate circle—undeniable. What

Dave should have realized is that all of that press and gossip were making him more famous by association. Ed hated it, I hated it, because the emphasis was on something other than the music. But with the wisdom of forty years of hindsight, I can see that it was in our interest for more people to hear the name Van Halen. What do we care if you first heard of us reading about Ed and Valerie, the happy couple, in the checkout aisle in a gossip rag? If that's what got you to listen to our records, and you enjoy what we do, that's great. The more people who are exposed to our music, the more people we reach, the better. "I think it pissed him off because all of a sudden, I got a whole other side of the limelight that he wanted," Ed's said. "The tabloids and *People* magazine kind of shit—some people thrive on all that attention."

Now, *were* Ed and Valerie the happy couple, America's sweethearts, that they were made out to be? Listen, they didn't know what they were doing; they were kids. Though not as young as my dad imagined: when he first heard about Ed's new girlfriend, he watched some *One Day at a Time* to get a sense of her. Then he called Ed and said no way, he totally disapproved, he didn't want Ed marrying a fifteen-year-old. Ed had to explain to Dad that he'd been watching reruns.

They got engaged four months after they met, on New Year's Eve 1980. They started making preparations for a big Hollywood wedding, four or five hundred people, before they really even knew each other. Hell, at that age, they barely had a sense of themselves! "The priest we tapped to perform the ceremony gave us questionnaires so he could get to know us better and offer more personal words," Valerie wrote in one of her books. "As we filled out the forms at home, we each held a little vial of cocaine. Now, if you ask me, those are not two people who should be making decisions about the rest of their lives."

Hard to argue with that. But then, they stayed together for twenty-five years, so they must have gotten something right. Got married April 11, 1981, shortly before the release of *Fair Warning*. The ceremony was at Saint Paul's Catholic church—my mother was happy about that part. Ed was going to be a married man, and he was going to have a Catholic wife . . . and he was even going to wear a suit! Well, a white tuxedo. Close enough.

Nicolette Larson was Valerie's maid of honor. I was Ed's best man.

As far as I can remember, Dave didn't even bother to show up for the party.

SO NOW ED'S GOT A new bride. Dave has boycotted Ed's wedding celebration. And it's time to go on tour. It does not seem like the ideal time for us to be together twenty-four hours a day for months on end.

So how did we do on that tour?

Fantastic.

I can't explain it. All the conflict just drained away when we got onstage. The audience looks at you as something bigger than you actually are, and when you feel that energy coming at you from tens of thousands of people, it overpowers any petty crap you've got going on with your bandmates. Plus I'm in the zone! I'm playing. I'm not thinking about anything, I'm just going, going, going. When we were onstage, we were all in and in the moment. Ed put it this way: "When Dave, Al, Mike, and I get along great, it's no different than when we can't stand each other."

This is from the review of our sold-out show in Manhattan in July 1981, written by the famous critic Stephen Holden of the *New York Times*: "The music that is keeping the record business afloat is the heavy metal brand of hard rock established by Led Zeppelin in the late 1960's. And the triumphant appearance of Van Halen, one of the heaviest of heavy metal rock groups, at Madison Square Garden on Friday was impressive evidence." Personally, I don't think of Van Halen as heavy metal. But obviously I like it when people call us the American version of Zeppelin, in so many words. That's a comparison I'll take any day of the week. Holden went on to say that Ed "wielded his guitar like a lethal weapon."

ED LEFT OUR PARENTS' HOUSE before I did when he got married. I opted to stay in Pasadena and keep my dad company—it was obvious somebody had to besides our mom or he wouldn't be around much longer. He was bored out of his mind.

My mother didn't like being alone at night, so she discouraged him from going out and playing. Dad was just kind of falling apart, drinking a lot, even for him. I was trying to keep him entertained—without music, marriage wasn't enough.

Mikey got married not that long after Ed, to Sue, his high school sweetheart. They'd basically been married anyway. Other than his passion for Jack Daniel's, Mike was a pretty wholesome guy. While we were buying cars, he was collecting Mickey Mouse memorabilia. Van Halen played his wedding.

I tried it, too. Got married to a girl I'd been dating a couple years after Ed went down the aisle. (For a while we also had a second girl living with us. What was that like? *Busy.*) Two months after the wedding, we were already getting started on the divorce. So then I got married again a year later. You remember what Oscar Wilde said about second marriages? The triumph of hope over experience.

Third time's the charm. I'm not going to talk about the first two experiments because I don't feel like they count. I was practicing for Stine.

MUSIC LED ME TO HER.

Stine was working as an art director at Warner Bros. in the midnineties. I was the point man in the band for that kind of thing then. The first time I walked into her office, everything was clean, minimalist, except for an orange beanbag and a green jar of pickles on her desk. The way those two colors set each other off was so striking, such a reflection of Stine's vibrance as a person. Design for her wasn't just a job, it was a form of communication. She'd chosen those two objects because of the effect that juxtaposition would have on the viewer. In this case, me. And I was dazzled.

Stine was born in Copenhagen—my part of the world—and she comes from a family of artistic Jewish individualists. Talking to her that day, I felt like I was home. She understood me. We shared a way of looking at the world. The same things made us laugh. And then there was the miniskirt. Everything was just easy and exciting at the same time.

I owe that woman my life. She loved me enough—and was strong enough—to say, "I'm out of here," when she saw me slipping into addiction. I can still see her walking out the door with our cat in a box.

I got hooked on benzos on the tour in 1995. I wasn't sleeping; I was in a lot of pain. I have a vertebral injury from that accident on the boat with Gregg in the seventies, and it got to the point where if I moved in certain ways I'd be temporarily paralyzed. My neck was killing me, and without sleep, my body was falling apart. The tour manager gave me two Valiums and it was fantastic. Wow. It was the first time I'd slept in months! The relief was enormous.

So if two are good, then six must be . . .

By the time I got home I was totally addicted. I walked through life with my head in a fluffy cloud for six months. By then reality had become thoroughly dissipated. My experience with benzos gave me an understanding of Ed's monumental challenge to come.

Everyone from the business end of things was calling me, telling me what to do, how I should go about kicking the drugs. But it was entirely clear that they weren't trying to save me; they were trying to preserve their own incomes. The show must go on for everyone to get paid, and they needed me back out on the road. None of that helped.

Stine had lost her brother—who was a brilliant jazz drummer— to a heroin overdose. She knew the deal with addiction and the only way to get through to an addict. (Her brother, Stine says, was a lot like Ed: a prodigy who was given this incredible gift but struggled a great deal to function in the regular world—the hard stuff was easy for him, the easy stuff was hard.) Losing Stine was the only price I wasn't willing to pay for the drug.

Once I make my mind up about something, there's no stopping me. So, Stine moved back in with Emma—the cat, a wild thing from downtown LA. We had hell for four or five weeks while I was coming off the drugs, hallucinating, screaming, traveling to another dimension . . . and then being extremely concerned that

I'd left my shoes there, which I was convinced would create havoc, because obviously if you change something in another dimension, the ripple effects in your own dimension could be disastrous. I had gotten sober in '87 and I thought that was tough. But alcohol was nothing compared to getting off benzos.

When you are going through withdrawal, every piece of information that ever went into your brain gets just completely jumbled up. But you're not aware of that! It's not like acid, where you take it expecting to hallucinate. This just creeps up on you and you think it's real. I was hearing the same song over and over again in my head—Zeppelin, of course, I can't remember which one—and it was driving me *crazy*. Day in, day out, it just wouldn't stop. I was going around the house with a tape recorder trying to record it and asking Stine, "Do you hear it? Do you hear it?" I distinctly remember being on the staircase, going down to get a gun to shoot myself—not because I wanted to die, just to make the music stop. And halfway down the steps the song stopped playing. I was free.

Eventually, I found a way to protect myself—from fame, from the music business, from drugs and alcohol. With Stine I was able to carve out a home, a zone that had nothing to do with work or fame.

Ed was never able to create that.

THIRTEEN

For art to exist, for any sort of aesthetic activity or
perception to exist, a certain physiological precondition
is indispensable: intoxication.

—*Friedrich Nietzsche*

Neuroscientists talk about convergent and divergent thinking:
the two kinds of thinking that contribute to creativity. Divergent
thinking is about searching for originality, letting your brain roam
free in the hopes that you'll arrive somewhere new. Brainstorm-
ing. You throw out a lot of stuff and see what hits the wall; you
are open to the paths your mind wants to roam. You can arrive at
far-out ideas in that state that may seem unrelated to each other,
that are shooting all over the place and intersecting like the lines
on Ed's guitar. He had a gift for this kind of thinking. And I had
a gift for backing him up on it—rhythmically and emotionally.
Together, we were generative. We were making music out of
thin air.

The creative process requires this, obviously, but it also entails *con*vergent thinking, which is about synthesizing, consuming lots of ideas and inspirations and incorporating them. Dave was good at this. Some fans made a documentary about us and they interviewed one of Dave's good friends from school, who put it well: "You have to get it from somewhere . . . and if you don't have it within, you have to get it from whatever is around you." Dave took in all sorts of insane stuff from cartoons and books, movies and musicals, and then put his own distinctive twist on them. We encouraged him to do what he wanted a lot of the time and humored his crazy ideas because we wanted *all* of him—his whole soul—all in. I didn't just want him to be the clown!

We knew that his energy created this contrapuntal force that set what Ed and I did off, the way two colors at opposite ends of the spectrum accentuate each other. You put orange next to green and both colors scream at you in a way that's kind of exciting. And if you find just the right shade of each, you've got something elegant and interesting, too—a contrast with some sophistication. That's what we were going for.

But I think (I know) that Dave was angry at Ed for being so talented. I actually think he sold himself short by competing with Ed. Just appreciate your *own* gift! *We* do! The bottom line is that Dave desperately wanted to be an artist but something was always missing. He could never really *feel* the music, it was all cerebral. He didn't get the part where you need to resonate with something deeper, something like the eternal force of the universe. *That's* how you make art. You clear away your ego and try to shut off the thinking, calculating part of your brain. You can't make a *plan* to touch a dragon's tail.

To my mind, there was never enough depth behind Dave's passing enthusiasms. He seemed to think that a costume change was
all it took. I recently saw the movie *Barbie* (loved it, by the way).
You know how there's Doctor Barbie, Cowgirl Barbie, President
Barbie, and so on? That's kind of how it was for Dave: Leather
Dave, Karate Dave, Director Dave, whatever. "Inspiration doesn't
come from nowhere," Dave once told Martha Quinn (remember
her?!) on MTV. "You don't lay in a dark black room and suddenly
a burst of light and the hand of the Lord comes out and says
'Here, have a song.' It doesn't happen like that. You have to steal
it from somebody."

I think Dave deeply envied that for Ed, it *did* happen like
that. I'm not saying Ed didn't work for his inspiration; all he did
was play guitar. And I'm not saying he didn't have influences: he
learned from Clapton, from Holdsworth and Beethoven, just like
I learned from Ginger Baker and Hal Blaine. But he had flashes
of genuine ingenuity, moments of originality that could only have
come from Ed—or *through* Ed, I should say. Because the really
great stuff comes from somewhere else.

The problem is that being human, when everybody loves what
you just did, you want to do it again. And again. "Sometimes I
freak myself out, I go, *Whoa, that was kind of magical.* But those
kind of things you can't always count on," Ed said. "An inspira-
tional, spur-of-the-moment thing, you think, *Wow, how'd I do
that?* I try to do it again . . . and I can't."

You want to recapture it; it's frustrating and painful when it
eludes you. So you try to re-create the exact conditions from the
time when the magic happened. You do everything the same: you
eat the same thing for breakfast, put your right shoe on before

your left, snort the same number of lines. Musicians tend to be superstitious in general, and we were raised by a mother from the islands: islanders are the most superstitious people on the planet. (We were never supposed to leave a glass completely empty, for example—Mom taught us to always leave something in there to maintain balance.) You can spend your whole life trying to make what happened before happen again. I honestly believe that's what cost my brother his life.

Drugs and alcohol were very much a part of the early years when we exploded into American consciousness. So going back to them again and again was partly an attempt to return to the original formula. Just the right amount of intoxication can open "the doors of perception," to borrow Aldous Huxley's phrase. Huxley wrote about the way the brain filters the vast quantities of stimuli that come in every second of every day through our eyes, hands, mouths, noses, and, most important to us, ears. At any given moment we are inundated with so much information that if we didn't block some out, we'd never be able to get anything done and we'd probably go completely crazy. We have what Huxley called a "reducing valve" that blurs out what we don't need.

But to make music or art, sometimes (a lot of the time) you need to disable the reducing valve and let everything roll in. You need to feel it all, hear it all. You need a different kind of access to your own senses and sensitivities. So how do you get that? You take in whatever you can find, whatever works for you personally, to alter your consciousness.

What you've got to do is let your mind just *go*. And when you take drugs, the critical part of your brain is gone. You stop thinking, *I can't do that because it's never been done.* All that stuff goes out the window. If somebody else says, "Don't even bother with that," it doesn't matter. It's irrelevant. Because now you can just go with the flow. That's why so many creative people try drugs. You've got to shut out the voices that inhibit you from experimenting and just *experience* your art. ("Are you experienced? Have you ever been experienced? Well, I have." There's a reason he called it the Jimi Hendrix Experience.)

Now, there are plenty of ways to reach this state: neuroscientists see the same patterns in the brains of experienced meditators as they do in users of psychedelics. But we hadn't really been exposed to meditation. The only way Ed and I knew of to stop time and let the universe into our music was to consume intoxicants.

Unfortunately, right in the middle of that word, hiding in plain sight, is another word: "toxic."

BY THE END OF '81, we'd basically been on the road or in the studio for four straight years. We were spent after the *Fair Warning* tour; none of us wanted to do another record right away. We wanted to catch our breath. And Ed was a newlywed! So to slow everything down without completely disappearing, we decided we'd start '82 by releasing a single instead of a new album.

The previous summer, MTV had launched. The very first video they aired was "Video Killed the Radio Star" by the Buggles. Prescient! Right out of the gate they're announcing: *Here is the beginning of the end of music for its own sake. The video has arrived and nothing will ever be the same.* Those Buggles had it exactly right: "In my mind and in my car / We can't rewind we've gone too far / Pictures came and broke your heart / Put the blame on VCR." I do! VCRs and MTV robbed people of the freedom to experience music and invent their own mental images and associations.

Naturally, Dave wanted to create "the most lavish home movie ever made" and get it on the air. And that was early on, so I'm sure we all felt like videos were a novelty, something different we could try that might be fun. We didn't understand what was coming.

We decided we'd do a cover since the video was really the point. Dave wanted "Dancing in the Street." Ed wanted to do "Pretty Woman." Dave was very shrewd about things like this—he probably caved to Ed because he knew that way Ed wouldn't back out of doing the video altogether. (Take a look at Ed's face in our first video and you'll have a pretty good sense of how happy he was about the whole event!)

The concept was simple: damsel in distress; Van Halen to the rescue. Only, because it was us, everything had to be twisted. The damsel was a guy in a dress (with great legs, by the way). The distress was that she'd been captured and tied to some poles and we were four different archetypal heroes showing up to save her: Mikey was a samurai; I was a shirtless Tarzan type in a loincloth—and a pair of aviator sunglasses! HA! Ed was a cowboy, and Dave was Napoleon with more makeup on his face than the guy in the wig.

We released our video in early '82. Within weeks, it was banned. First in Japan, and then in Australia. It offended their delicate sensibilities; we weren't welcome on the airwaves. Bad news, right? Not for us. The whole thing generated a ton of press, and suddenly we're not just the guys who play loud music, have drunken food fights, and hate brown M&M's, we're victims of censorship! We're champions of free speech! I love America.

Our version of "Pretty Woman" started climbing the charts. Good news, right? Not for us. Because now that we've got a hit, Warner Bros. wants to profit from it. And for that to happen, they need a record to sell—right away, before the song is off the radio.

They insisted that we rush-record one immediately to chase the single. "We're going wait a minute, we just *did* that to keep us out there, so people knew we were still alive," Ed told Jas Obrecht in an '82 interview, "but they just kept pressuring, 'We need that album, we need that album,' so we jumped right back in, without any rest, without any time to recuperate from the tour, and started recording." Instead of pausing the annual cycle of recording and touring, we'd managed to expedite it.

How do you make a record with no time and no songs? You do a bunch of cover tunes. Now, you remember how sick we were of playing covers back in the *clubs*. So nobody was happy with the way our fifth album came about. "A lot of stuff on *Diver Down* we just threw together," Ted admitted. "It's no surprise that we ended up doing five covers. As their producer, that frustrated me . . . we just didn't have enough time to work on the record."

The other drag on us was that Dave had become increasingly negative about (a.k.a. jealous of) Ed's status within the music world, and he expressed it by discouraging Ed's ideas and telling him "Enough with the solos" whenever he had the chance. In Ed's telling: "One day when Dave wasn't there, I said, 'Ted, what do you think of this? What do you think of that?' I played him 'Little Guitars,' the intro, the little flamenco-sounding thing, and 'Cathedral,' and he's going like, 'God! Why the fuck didn't you show me this earlier?' And I explained to him, Dave just said, 'Fuck the guitar hero shit, you know, we're a *band*.'"

Ted had more appreciation than Dave did for the epic value of Ed's guitar solos on our records. That's the good news. The bad news is that Ted had his own blind spot that had to do, understandably, with his allegiance to Warner Bros. . . . he just happened to be *dead wrong*.

Here's what I'm talking about. Ed came up with the chord progression for "Jump"—our biggest hit, our only number one single, an anthem that has become iconic all over the world and will probably outlive everything else we did—in 1982. (It evolved out of the intro to "Hear About It Later," a song Ed wrote for *Fair Warning*—it's basically the same chord progression, the same theme, just sped up and reorchestrated.) Ed played it for everyone hoping we'd get it on *Diver Down*. Dave thought it was lame. And after all his complaints about the guitar hero shit, Dave had the audacity to tell Ed he shouldn't be playing another instrument: "You're a guitar hero, nobody wants to hear you play keyboards." *Well, which is it, Dave? Pick a lane!*

The craziest thing is that Ted agreed with him! *He never liked the sound of "Jump."* I'm sorry, but if you hear those chords and they don't move you, you're not *alive*. It's like Beethoven's Fifth! *Dun dun dun DUN.* It's just an iconic series of notes that you can't unhear. "I thought, 'How can you ignore this?'" Donn said about Ted's not wanting to record the song.

Think about the opening of "Jump." Can *you* imagine hearing that and thinking, *Nah, there's nothing there. Next*?

You'd think Ted, a "platinum producer," a senior VP at Warner Bros., would be embarrassed that he didn't immediately know a massive hit when he heard it! Instead, he's still knocking it forty years later: "This riff sounds like keyboard playing you'd hear between innings at a baseball stadium," he said in his book. *It's called an anthem, for crying out loud!* "When Van Halen uses keyboards, they should sound nasty like they do on 'And the Cradle Will Rock,' or 'Sunday Afternoon in the Park.' They should shatter your senses and make your ears bleed." *Ted! It's* music. *If it sounds good, it is good!*

So there was all that friction. And on top of that, we were all demoralized and exhausted; we had no desire to rush out on tour, and more covers were the last thing we wanted to put out there. "I hated every minute of making it," Ed said of *Diver Down*. "C'mon, Van Halen doing 'Dancing in the Street'? It was stupid. I started feeling like I would rather bomb playing my own songs than be successful with someone else's." For the record jacket, we picked the red and white flag that goes up to indicate there are divers swimming deep beneath the surface: a recycled image for a record of recycled songs.

On the back cover of *Diver Down* we put a picture I've always loved, of the four of us onstage saying goodbye to a sea of fans at the end of a show. Take a look: big audience, right? Well, yeah, because it's a Stones audience! HA! It was from the afternoon we opened for the Rolling Stones in Orlando, in October '81. Yet another example of our marketing genius. (We got permission from them to use it, obviously, and we played our guts out for that crowd, as you can see from that picture.)

Wouldn't you know it: *Diver Down* outsold *Fair Warning*. Did better on the charts, topping out at number three. For the first time, due to Dave's influence, there weren't any guitar solos on half the songs. Ed was so upset about it all—the fights with Ted over "Unchained," the fights with Dave over, well, everything—that he wanted to dissolve the band. There were times we'd get into fistfights about it backstage. "Are you crazy?" I told him. "After all the work we've done to get here?" I thought that if we threw it all away it would be an enormous mistake and that Dave would walk away holding all the marbles.

There was one inarguably great thing about *Diver Down*: we got our dad to play on it. It was Dave's idea to cover "Big Bad Bill

(Is Sweet William Now)." He had this Walkman, and you could record on those if you heard something you liked while you were listening to the radio. "In a certain spot in his room, if he pointed the antenna a certain way, he'd pick up this weird . . . I don't know *what* you'd call that kind of music," Ed told Jas Obrecht. "He played it to us, and we just started laughing ourselves silly. I'm going, 'This is bad! Let's do it!'" It was such an unexpected style of song for us—we all got a kick out of how funny it would be to have a quintet from the thirties on a Van Halen album. It was also Dave's idea to have our father play the clarinet on that tune. Dave's intentions may have been strategic, but I don't care what motivated him. I'll always be grateful to Dave for coming up with that. The result was very cool.

My dad was past his prime and dying to get out of the house. This was a great way for him to be included in the life of the band, and, of course, our music. It was a very humbling experience recording with him. He was getting very uneasy, and now it was our turn to walk him through a professional experience. We'd spent our lives looking up to him, having him explain the way everything worked when it came to playing . . . when it came to everything! And now the shoe was on the other foot. "He was nervous as shit, and we're just telling him, 'Jan, just fucking have a good time! Man, we make mistakes, that's what makes it real,'" Ed said. "I *love* what he did. It's just that he's thinking back ten years ago, when he was smokin', playing jazz and stuff. He just can't do it anymore because he's wearing dentures. Whenever you're playing a wind instrument you gotta keep the muscle tone of your lips in shape, and your teeth have a lot to do with it too, and when you're wearing dentures and missing a finger . . . it's like we almost had to force him to do it. But fuck, it's exactly what we wanted." We tried to get him to come onstage with us when we played LA, but Dad refused.

Listening to his clarinet—to the whole song—is pretty special for me. It's the only really good recording out there of all three Van Halen men playing music together.

By then, my dad's nose had changed color from the alcohol. Had we known about AA, we could have gotten him in a program, but that was completely foreign to us at that point; we didn't know anything about the twelve steps. He was disintegrating, declining, before our eyes. After Dad had a heart attack in 1986, he told me, "Alex, I don't want to be here anymore."

I wanted to deck him, to be completely honest. *You don't get to die yet, you're only sixty-six! And* I *still need you around.* As far as I'm concerned, when you become a father, you give up your right to die early. There are times when I've been in so much pain I've wanted to exit stage left, but I have two sons: I'm not going anywhere by choice. You bring another person into this world, I think the least you can do is stick around for them as long as possible.

But my father was in bad shape. A lifetime of drinking had destroyed his body and wasn't doing great things for his mind. His organs started giving out, and he died a few months later. Dad got his wish.

I was devastated. We went into the studio, Mikey was there, and we just played for four or five hours nonstop. It was the only thing we knew to do to try to cope with our grief.

I completely came apart. Alcohol became more fraught and complicated than ever for me. On the one hand, I'm sad and maybe even angry that my dad basically drank himself to death. Suddenly alcohol is revealing itself as this poison, this thing that can kill you, kill your father, ruin your life. On the other hand, drinking is what my dad and I did together. I miss the hell out of the guy, I'm never going to see him again, and this is the way we communed. What else am I going to do? Besides music and blood, alcohol was the most impactful thing we shared.

Looking back, I realize I was drinking from the moment I got up to the moment I went to sleep.

The night before Ed married Val. We sat there drinking white wine with my dad until we couldn't talk anymore . . . which was not unusual.

ED BEFORE

And they said it wouldn't last!

ED AFTER

A promotional tour in Europe.
There were excuses to party all day long.

A few sheets to the wind!
There's a lot of dead time on the road.

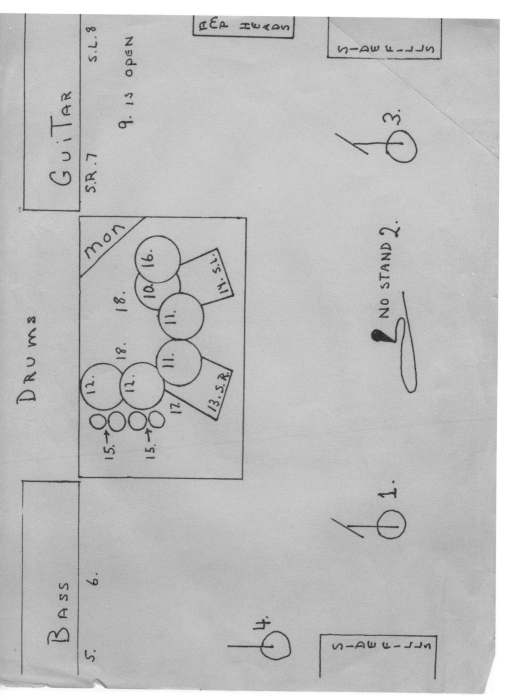

Layout for the stage, mid-'70s.

Ed's room in what I call "the real house": the place we bought for my parents in 1979.

Playing in Mammoth with Mark Stone *(far right)*, the '70s.

In-store
appearance.

$2.75 to see a
show in 1977 . . .
those were
the days.

A fan's car in Holland on our second tour.
The Van Halen virus was beginning to spread.

Ed and me in Mexico in 1979. It was
Dave's idea that we should all go to Club Med.
We had a blast. This was right before I won a
windsurfing contest. And a drinking contest.

Fooling around on our instruments
in the living room on Las Lunas
Street. That was all we ever did.

12/26/77

Alex Van Halen agrees to pay the
sum of 20.00 (twenty dollars) to
Cosmic Lighting for the rental of
one smoke machine for the use
of it at the Wiskey night club
Hollywood on the date of 12/31/77.
Alex Van Halen takes all responsibilites
for the care and return of the
smoke machine and agrees to pay for
any damages that may happen during
rental period.

pick up date 12/26/77
return date 1/2/78

cosmic lighting

Alex Van Halen

Gotta have a contract! We learned this when a Catholic
school refused to pay us because they said they'd
smelled pot at our gig. So we went to court. And the
judge had just one question for the nuns: How do
you know what pot smells like? Case dismissed!

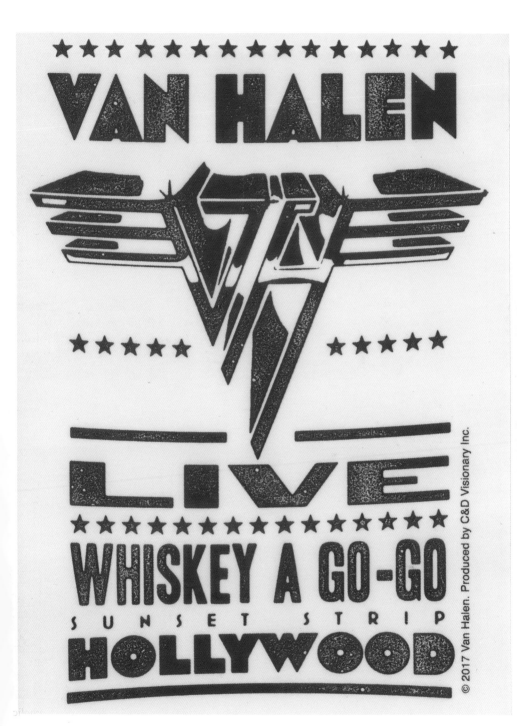

Starting in the spring of 1974, the Sunset Strip was our hunting ground.

Mom and Dad: love prevails.

Ed and Al: always together. *(© Lynn Goldsmith / Getty Images)*

FOURTEEN

I don't know what's going to happen in the future,
maybe somebody else in the band will get egoed out
or something. But I'd love Van Halen to be forever . . .
I'm getting hit up left and right now: "Will you play on
my record, will you do this, will you do that?" And I go,
"No, Van Halen is my family. I'm not gonna wash your
dishes. I'll wash dishes for Van Halen alone."

—*Edward Van Halen, in* Guitar Player, *1980*

There were very few things that we did apart. The
assumption was that anything I was doing he was doing,
and vice versa, especially when it came to music. Any
deviation from that was unpleasant.

—*Me, 164 pages ago*

So back in 1980, based on the quote above, Ed got the concept:
when you're in a band, all of your efforts should go toward it. It's

never going to work if you dissipate your energy going in a dozen different directions. For a band to succeed, everyone in it has to be focused on propelling that entity forward, as a shared mission. That's how we got to where we were.

But then Ed got a call from Quincy Jones in '82 asking him to play on Michael Jackson's record, and suddenly all of that went out the window. He asked me if I thought he should do it, and I said, "No! Use your head: they want you so they can broaden Jackson's appeal. If you want to broaden our appeal, Jackson should be on our record! It's not in Van Halen's interest for you to be playing with other acts. Why would you burn up what creativity you have on someone else when we're only given so much?"

It's not like we'd never been through any of this in the past. When we were making our second record, Ted was simultaneously producing Nicolette Larson's, and he asked Ed to play guitar on some of the tracks. Dave wouldn't have it. "I got right between them, I said, 'No way! You're not going to run off with bits and pieces of the scenery before the play starts,'" Dave declared. "Ed wanted to play on it. I said, 'Great. But you got to put a question mark on where your name goes. Got to keep it all in one camp.'" Ed understood that back then and he acceded. You can hear him unmistakably on some of the tracks on *Nicolette*, but his name is nowhere to be found on the record.

An ensemble has to be all for one and one for all—or it'll fall apart. The Michael Jackson thing was no different. "Whether you like it or not, you're a valuable commodity, Ed," I told him. "You're being traded by other people, and you're not getting anything out of it. And neither is the band."

"Okay," Ed says. "I get it. You're right."

I go away for the weekend, and when I get back, I find out he did it anyway!

I was furious! We had a huge fight . . . and then smaller versions of the same fight for years afterward because the consequences of the whole thing were so far-reaching. I couldn't understand what he was thinking. *Dad taught us: everything you do in this life, you should do with laser focus. A light shining all over the place is just a blur. But focus it down to a laser beam and it can cut through a door.*

Why would you diffuse your energy?!? Inspiration is finite.

"I was only in the studio for an hour," Ed tells me. "I didn't even get paid; it's no big deal. And who's even heard of this kid anyway?"

"You are in the fucking music business, Ed! And you're asking who's going to hear it?!"

"Beat It" went number one all over the world. Ed's cameo on *Thriller* became one of the most famous solos in rock . . . *and it wasn't on a Van Halen record.* It wasn't *just* a solo, either: Ed had actually rearranged the whole track. ("I listened to the song, and I immediately go, 'Can I change some parts?' I turned to the engineer and I go, 'Okay, from the breakdown, chop in this part, go to this piece, pre-chorus, to the chorus, out.' Took him maybe ten minutes to put it together. And I proceeded to improvise two solos over it," Ed admitted on television.) Ed's musical contribution to "Beat It" was pretty substantial.

He didn't even warn Dave it was coming. "Beat It" dropped in early '83, just after we got back from the South American leg of the *Diver Down* Hide Your Sheep Tour. (Tagline: "Where men are men and sheep are scared!") When Dave heard it on the radio, his first thought was that someone was knocking off my brother.

I think when he realized it was really Ed, he felt betrayed. And honestly, the way Ed went about it, so did I.

Look, Ed's my brother, and I'm always going to take his side. But this gave Dave a leg to stand on when *he* wanted to do things without the rest of the band. It amped up the game of tit for tat between my brother and Dave—it's not like it started with the Michael Jackson thing. It was ongoing and intensifying:

Dave was mad at Ed for upstaging him in the press with Valerie.

Ed was mad at Dave for blowing off his wedding party.

Dave was mad at Ed for being a musical prodigy—for getting attention as an individual, a virtuoso, separate from Van Halen.

Ed was mad at Dave for putting up a fight about almost every instrumental track on our records.

And on and on, about matters large and small, creative and technical, sonic and visual, intellectual and moronic.

ED DID ANOTHER SIDE PROJECT around the same time that was a hell of a lot more discreet than playing on *Thriller*, but it ended up being equally consequential. He'd befriended Frank Zappa, who lived near him in Coldwater Canyon, where Ed had moved in with Valerie. Ed got to know Frank's twelve-year-old son Dweezil over there, too, and man, was he good to him. Ed gave Dweezil one of his own guitars and taught him a few songs on it. ("Of course I asked Edward to play 'Mean Street' and 'Eruption,'" Dweezil said. "I got to watch it up close. The techniques he employed were burned into my brain forever.") But get this: Ed and Donn agreed to produce Dweezil's first single—the kid's in junior high school! I don't know what possessed them! We had a huge fight about it . . . "What the hell are you thinking?! First you want to solo on someone else's record and now you want to produce a frigging twelve-year-old?! Just because his dad says you've reinvented the guitar?? Have you lost your mind?" At least they had the good sense to keep their names off it. It said on the record that it was produced by "the Vards" . . . a play on my mother's pronunciation of Ed*vard*.

Frank Zappa had been on Warner Bros. himself for eight years. He left on a sour note because he felt constrained creatively, an experience that was becoming all too familiar to us. Ever since then, Frank had been working from home at his own studio. While Ed and Donn were making Dweezil's single there, they became aware of a few things.

At a home studio, you can spend as long as you want noodling around, recording, listening to what you've done, tweaking it, and so on. You're not paying by the hour for studio space, and your producer can't pressure you accordingly. You can customize your studio to your own taste and requirements—there are a million little decisions you can make to personalize it, make it uniquely suited to your preferences as a musician. Maybe best of all, you can work in your studio anytime, day or night, whenever inspiration strikes. If it's 4 a.m. and you want to record something, you can just roll out of bed and start working . . . and Ed had become basically nocturnal. (This wasn't great for his wife, who had to be on set at a reasonable hour. I'm sure it gets aggravating being married to a bat.)

After spending a few weeks at Zappa's, Ed came away convinced: the only way to have real freedom was to build his own studio in Coldwater Canyon. And now that he was married to a very wealthy network television star, that was entirely achievable. (A side note about their house and their wealth: Around the time they got married, my mom went over to see where her son was going to be living. Valerie had a lot of antiques. After our mom left, she called Ed and said, "Can't you afford some new furniture? I can loan you the money.")

Valerie was into building a studio. We were on the road so much, I'm sure she liked the idea that when Ed was home, he could actually *be* home, and not away all the time at Sunset Sound or Amigo Studios. Ed and Valerie took turns on a Caterpillar knocking down a section of the old guesthouse to make room for us.

Drew, one of the Nellies, had lived in there with his girlfriend for a while. He was in construction, so we figured we'd give him the job of building the studio to make up for the fact that we'd commandeered his house. Donn designed it, and Drew built it with this guy Ron Fry, who came up with a really good solution to our biggest obstacle. You couldn't get a permit to build a studio on a residential property. But Ron said, hey: a studio can't have windows; it has to be soundproof. Let's get a permit for a *racquetball court* and then transform it. (The authorities didn't think twice about handing out permits for racquetball courts. It was the eighties; every celebrity was building one of those damn things.) So, they got the permit, they built the court, and for about three weeks we played racquetball. The court just happened to have concrete walls thick enough to keep out any sound bleed from the fifty-thousand-watt radio tower a few miles away. Ed was always good at retrofitting things—guitars, cars—so it felt appropriate that he should have a studio that began its life as something else.

"We did it for no money," Donn told me recently. "The history of home studios in those days was basically guys would spend tons of money, and then they'd make records that didn't sell, and this studio would become a terrible burden. I didn't want that to happen." He knew that even though we'd sold millions of records, we were still not where we should have been financially; we were still putting all our money back into the band. You might think I'm exaggerating but that was honestly our reality: the money wasn't great. "I got a sixteen-track recorder for four thousand dollars," Donn recalled. "The console was from 1961. We had a budget of fifty thousand dollars for everything—all the equipment, tape machines, microphones, everything in the studio—and we came in under." When they were building 5150, the idea was still just that we'd have a clubhouse, a place we could experiment. "We didn't think we'd do anything of real significance in there," Donn said, and that's my memory, too. "And then, of course, we made a quite successful record."

Ed did the decorating: there was a double-layer window between the tiny control room and the main studio, and in between the two panes of glass, Ed entombed a piranha he'd brought back from Argentina and stuck a cigarette in its mouth. He made it perfectly clear: at this studio, there's no nonsmoking section. More often than not, Ed had one cigarette in his mouth, a second one stuck at the end of his guitar, and yet another burning away in the ashtray that he'd forgotten about.

One day his friend Steve Lukather, the guitarist from Toto, came by to see the place. Ed's giving him the tour: this is going to be the control room; here's the studio; and oh! This is where I keep my gun! Ed had a new .44 Magnum—which, if you know anything about guns, is just a ridiculous choice for self-defense, it's like a *cannon*. Well, Ed was used to a Colt, but this was a Smith & Wesson, and the cylinder turns in the opposite direction on those, so when he looked at the cylinder and he didn't see a bullet, he assumed it wasn't loaded. Long story short, KA-BOOM. Ed blew a hole right through the concrete wall; the bullet came out the other side.

Donn came up with an apt name for the place: 5150. It's the police code for involuntary confinement of a mental patient who's a danger to himself or the community. (Donn was living in Malibu at the time, and he was always listening to his scanner to keep track of the wildfires up in the mountains, so he was learning all the police codes.) Everyone was telling us we were insane to build a studio when we had access to world-class facilities in Los Angeles. Calling it 5150 was our way of claiming the space as our own personal lunatic asylum.

As you can imagine, when we started working there, things did get crazy. To say that there were power struggles in the recording of our next album—our biggest record, our best record ever if you ask me—is the understatement of the century.

ONCE 5150 WAS UP AND RUNNING, we started working all hours of the day and, of course, night. It was fun there! The whole vibe was relaxed, we didn't run a clock. Most nights I'd stay there till three in the morning, and Donn and Ed would often keep going after I went home. (Remember: I was the one who didn't do coke!) There was nobody there to tell us keyboards were a bad idea or that Van Halen is supposed to be heavy metal. It was really free, the way it was in our bands as kids, where we could just experiment and jam for as long as we wanted.

Ed and Donn had become close friends but all three of us got along great and had a real mind meld going. We had the time and space to do whatever weird thing we wanted: Donn put little microphones all over Ed's Lamborghini, for instance, because we thought we might use the sound of the engine idling—it ended up on "Panama." Then there was "Stereo Septic": Drew Bertinelli left all kinds of crap in the guesthouse that we needed to get rid of, and right near us on the property was a big hole that used to house the septic tank before they switched over to using the sewer system. We thought, *Hmm, what can we fit in there?* And one day we dumped all of Drew's debris into the hole and Donn recorded it . . . I remember the Electrolux vacuum died a slow death and made some great sounds along the way.

We were actually microdosing acid while we worked on the album that became *MCMLXXXIV*—that's 1984!—to reach new places in our brains and our music. You know how everyone is saying now that psychedelics are so great for creativity? Based on our extensive experiments, I can tell you there's some truth to the rumor.

Ted wasn't thrilled with the situation: "It looked like a half-finished construction project on the inside. There were exposed two-by-fours and wires running everywhere. The patch bays weren't color-coded yet, so only Donn could decipher the inputs and outputs." Ted didn't like that he had less control over the process, and he was bummed out about its being smaller than the studios where he was used to recording. "Whenever I was in there, it felt like I was working in the bathtub—everything was so confined."

We didn't mind. We didn't need the big space we used to, because we didn't have to worry about isolating my drum kit so the sound wouldn't bleed onto other tracks during recording. I was working on a Simmons electronic kit now—the sound went directly into the console. Consequently, Ed and I could be jamming right up next to each other and Donn could record Ed's guitar track and my drums without worrying there would be any interference. (I get really irritated, by the way, when people complain about electronic drums . . . when you play an acoustic kit onstage or in a studio, a mic is what's transmitting the sound to the listener, so really, what you're hearing is electronic already! The only way you're really hearing the acoustic sound of a drum is when you're up pretty close to it. People hadn't really been hearing me play acoustic since we did parties at the Jewish Community Center in Pasadena.) In terms of the unfinished quality at 5150, that endured long after the studio was "finished." It didn't bother us. We're trying to be inventive in here! We'll be finished when we're *dead*.

5150 was a place where Ed felt liberated to create. "He was always soldering something or putting something together, making *some* sort of Frankenstein piece of gear," Steve Lukather remembers. "His workshop was always open; that was the first thing you'd see when you'd walk into 5150—there was his workbench with all of his tools and projects. He was always taking a neck off of something and putting it on something else or swapping out pickups. He was always looking for something new, even if he only got one song out of it. That's why he was Ed. He didn't do things the way everyone else does."

Donn told me recently that he still thinks "Jump" never would have been recorded without 5150; I know Ed felt the same way. "'Jump' was our only number one single, and believe it or not I built my studio to put that song on our record 'cause everyone hated it," my brother told Steve Baltin, yet another rock journalist. "Alex and I tracked the whole thing, certain people didn't want to be a part of it . . . I was always up against certain people saying, 'That doesn't sound like Van Halen' . . . well what *is* Van Halen? Van Halen is whatever I write because I write all the music."

It wasn't just "Jump" that Dave and Ted opposed. They were both against Ed playing keyboards in general. (Dave expressed his hostility for the synthesizer by referring to it as the "sympathizer.") They both had a preconceived idea about our sound that felt very constricting to us. "I said, 'Wait a minute. I signed a heavy metal band,'" Ted wrote. "I thought these guys should stay right in that pocket, and not go pop." *This from the guy who made us do "Dance the Night Away"?!*

And how many times do I have to say it? Van Halen is NOT a heavy metal band.

We're MUSICIANS!!!!!!!!!!!!!!!!!!!!!

Okay, I've calmed down.

But it was really irritating for Ed—for both of us—to be told not to evolve as an artist, not to try new instruments and ideas. Remember how we grew up? My father told us you can make music on a chair! The fun of it is innovating, *creating*. If you're lucky enough to have an idea for something that's different from everything you've already done? You grab it! Jesus, that's the whole point of what we do! This isn't Gazzarri's: we're not going to become a four-man jukebox that only plays Van Halen's "songs of the seventies."

We didn't think of it as "going pop." Ed was listening to a lot of classical music, actually, when he came up with the "Jump" riff. Listen, what's pop to me might be heavy metal to you. All these categories are really just marketing terms, not meaningful descriptions. I'll say it again: It's *music*. If it sounds good, it *is* good. That's what we were after: making something excellent.

And I think we achieved that on *1984*. It's the album that came closest to the sound we were always shooting for . . . it remains the record I'm proudest of and enjoy listening to the most. Same was true for Ed.

The album's original title was *Animal Farm*—we were on a real Orwell kick, and thinking a lot about power and control and the way human beings battle it out, because *we* were battling it out. "I came to realize that Ed, and Al too, had started seeing me less as a collaborator and more as the individual who wanted to limit their freedom to do what they wanted with the record," Ted wrote, and he wasn't wrong. It's ironic, really: Ed gives up piano to rebel against our mother; now he's reclaiming the keyboard and it's perceived as a rebellion by our producer.

Because we had 5150, we had all the time we wanted to perfect "Jump." Eventually, we converted Ted. ("Donn, working with Ed and Al, had gotten greatness down on tape," he conceded. Well, Ted, better late than never.) Then Ted had to go and convince Dave.

It was a massive pain in the ass getting Dave on board—"It was like pulling teeth to get him to sing the damn song," as Ed put it. But I have to hand it to Dave; when he finally stopped moaning and actually wrote the lyrics? He did a stellar job. (Initially, Ted was concerned Dave was writing a song encouraging suicide: *You want to kill yourself, sucker? Go ahead and jump.* According to Ted, Dave explained to him, "No, no, no! That's not what I mean, Teddy. I mean you've got to find your nerve. Take a chance! Ask that fine girl across the room to dance, even though she might say no. You're worried 'cuz she might turn you down, but life is all about rolling the dice and going for it—take a leap of faith and jump!" Hard to argue with that.) His lyrics were a perfect fit for those chords, that sound. Uplifting. Anthemic. "I get up and nothin' gets me down / You got it tough, I've seen the toughest around / And I know, baby, just how you feel / You got to roll with the punches to get to what's real." Soon, we'd be hearing tens of thousands of fans screaming those words back at us.

Robert Lombard had directed the "Pretty Woman" video for us. We liked him, and we wanted to work with him again on "Jump," but there was no way we were getting involved with the kind of elaborate production "Pretty Woman" entailed. Minimal, we told Lombard. Personal. That's what Ed and I were committed to. The video could be an embellishment on the music, an enhancement, but we weren't going to reverse the formula and spend more time making videos than making music.

Dave wasn't happy with a video that kept it simple. As far as he was concerned this was an opportunity to put more of his fantasies on film . . . and to boss a lot of people around in the process! "He wanted the performance video intercut with him doing crazy shit, like driving his chopped Merc hot rod and hanging out with midgets and girls in maid's outfits," Robert Lombard said. "So we shot hours of footage." It was all ridiculous and overblown and had everything to do with the carnival inside Dave's head, instead of anything to do with Van Halen. We ended up with the "Jump" video you know and love: a straightforward representation of us doing what we do best. But it was not an experience of comradery producing it. "I didn't shoot them together until the end of the day. I was trying to keep the peace because I felt tension amongst them," Lombard said.

Anyone who interacted with us experienced the strain in the band, and anyone could diagnose the reason: as Lombard put it, "David thought he was bigger than the rest of them."

ALL OUR OTHER ALBUMS WE made in a week or two. *1984* took almost a year. There were interruptions: we went to play the US Festival—and got paid a million and a half dollars to do it! (It seemed like a deranged amount of money at the time; it was totally unheard-of. We hoped it was the beginning of a new era in which Van Halen actually *made* money, instead of only earning it for other people.) Then we had to break so Ed could do the music for one of Valerie's TV movies, which none of us were thrilled about. But the main reason we took so long to make that record is that we *could*.

"Ed and I had a pact," Donn told me the last time I saw him. "'We're not going to puke this one out.' That was it, word for word. We would go in there and we'd work till we had it." They'd stay up for twenty-four hours, marathon sessions of playing and taping and tweaking. I guess it's the hazard as well as the benefit of having your own home studio: you can really forget about the rest of the world outside those walls.

As you can imagine, Valerie wasn't crazy about the way things were going—sure, Ed was on the premises, but it's not like he was coming into the house! "She was more concerned than anybody," Ted wrote. "She'd call me and say, 'Ted, they've been in there for two days. Can you come and get them out?'"

At that particular time, work was our idea of fun. Being totally exhausted and yet coming up with something terrific . . . it's a good time. What was the incentive to stop? "And we could always collapse on the floor," Donn said. "We did that a few times. Wake up and go, 'Where were we last night? Oh, right: *here*.' We just wanted every song to be as good as it could possibly be." 5150 was like our own little kingdom where we made all the rules. What else does a guy in his twenties want? What else does *anyone* want?

Dave was getting more and more pissed off. He wasn't about to stay up all night in there—not that he was particularly welcome. There were times during daylight hours when Ed would *have* to crash, and Dave would want to work. He was used to acting like it was his band, and there was no way to pretend that was the case anymore, now that Ed was in charge of the recording process.

Ed owned the studio, so we could control the mix, too, and finally—finally!—get the heft we'd always wanted, that thundering, Zeppelin-like hugeness of sound. It's very hard to put into words what we were after: if you could put sound into words, you wouldn't need sound! But Ed and I always had the same thing in mind: music that sounds "like Godzilla waking up" as Ed said. And Donn finally understood our goal. If it wasn't for Donn being flexible and taking the time to listen and poke around and do things differently, we never would have gotten *1984*.

It wasn't easy for him, I know: Donn was torn between his good friend Ed, a once-in-a-generation talent who he wanted to support, and Ted, the producer and Warner Bros. vice president who was Donn's employer. "I'd been with Warner Bros. for fifteen years and I'd done maybe thirty albums with Ted Templeman," Donn told me. "I let that go because this was just more important."

Unfortunately, Ted couldn't stand the sound we loved—the brown sound we finally achieved on *1984*. ("I thought the drums were too loud, and I said so. But Al wanted the drums to be higher and higher in the mix, and Donn and Ed agreed with him," Ted complained. "When we mixed, those three guys became of one mind.") He had different taste and that's legitimate. I'm not even saying he had bad taste—look at all the great records produced by Ted Templeman! I fully understand that Ted's got twenty bands to worry about, and twenty different new albums to produce at any given time, and that's not easy. But we only have one band, and it's our entire life.

This is our *voice*. If Ed had to build a studio to get it on tape, if we had to sneak around with Donn, if we had to overrule Ted and Dave, whatever it took, we were going to make an album that sounded like us to *us*.

THE PROOF IS IN THE RESULT. *1984* sold over ten million copies. *Rolling Stone* called it "the album that brings all of Van Halen's talent into focus." "Jump" was nominated for three Grammy awards. Apparently, Ted eventually conceded to Donn that *1984* was to Van Halen what *Sgt. Pepper* was to the Beatles: a full flowering of the band's creativity. The work of musicians who had a mature understanding of what they wanted and simply weren't going to stop until they achieved it.

1984 reached number two on the *Billboard* chart and stayed there for five weeks.

Want to take a guess why it didn't go to number one?

There was another album in the way.

Thriller.

FIFTEEN

Alex is usually overlooked, but he's a brilliantly musical drummer, almost as responsible as his brother for the heart-stopping power of "Jump." A few years ago, after the band was asked to open a date for the Rolling Stones in Florida before some 150,000 people, he broke his hand in four places. He couldn't even hold a drumstick. So he tied the stick to his wrist with a shoelace and went on with the show.

—Rolling Stone *magazine, 1984*

A writer from *Rolling Stone* came on our sold-out tour in early '84, and something stands out to me now when I reread that article, "Van Halen's Split Personality." I think my brother took my (first) divorce after two months of marriage harder than I did! "If I could suck the pain out of Alex I would," Ed told the reporter . . . and cried! "There are too many people on this basketball that's floating around the sun who are too afraid to allow themselves to feel," he went on. ". . . Hey, goddamnit, I'll cry if I want to, I'll get horny if I want to, I'll laugh, whatever. I'm incapable of holding things in." *Yeah, Ed, especially after a bottle of Blue Nun!*

I'll say it again: he was sensitive. Drunk or sober, happy or sad, the world just got right to him. Ed transmitted all that emotion through his music, his smile, his tears. Life just took him by storm. After *1984*, the strife with Ted and Dave depleted him. (Apparently, my divorce didn't help, either! HA!) Ed just wanted all that conflict to disappear.

And soon, after our biggest tour, for our best record, promoting our only number one single, it did.

IT STARTED WITH DAVE TELLING us he was going to do a solo EP— and that Ted was going to produce it. After all the crap you gave Ed about "Beat It," about his guitar solos in general, you're going to do your own record?! You can't be serious, Dave! It just seemed insane, preposterous. (And speaking of preposterous, without us to reel him in, Dave's musical taste went to hell in a handbasket as far as I'm concerned.)

Next thing we know he's written a screenplay. He called it *Crazy from the Heat*. Same name he gave his EP and his memoir . . . he couldn't get enough of that title. What's it about? DAVE!! A rock star named David Lee Roth who goes to the Dongo Islands with his entourage of freaks for madcap tropical adventures. You want to see a two-hour version of his "California Girls" video? This is it! He had the audacity to tell Ed he'd let us score it. That was the last conversation they had for a while.

It was arrogance. He got it in his head that we were holding him back instead of the reality, which was that we were all propelling each other forward. We were greater than the sum of our parts.

Rage is always there for me, and I had plenty of that while Dave was peeling off from the band . . . a little at a time, until one day . . . *Holy shit: did that clown just quit?!* It's like that Hemingway quote about how you go bankrupt: "Two ways. Gradually, then suddenly." That was the end of the original Van Halen.

I was angry but I was also confounded: We're at the peak of our career, things are finally getting to the level we've been dreaming of since we were teenagers, and you want to change the formula *now*? Do you have any idea how lucky we are, Dave? How rare this is? We finally sound like *us*!

WHAT ARE YOU THINKING???????

"When I left Van Halen, it was not something that I was delighted to do," Dave said a dozen years after he quit the band. "I was not celebrating. I was not relieved. It was one of the scariest moments in my life." Hindsight is 20/20. At the time, Dave had gotten himself a film deal with CBS and he was convinced his career as a writer/director/actor was going to make his start in the music business look dull by comparison. Then the film deal fell through. And he never got another one.

I'm not gloating. I don't take any pleasure in admitting that all of us were better together, no matter how much we fought, no matter how pissed off it makes me to think about it. "When Dave quit the band, Alex, Mike, and I were just pretty devastated," Ed said a few years later, after the fury had worn off. "We were just sitting there going, *Now what?* Here we've worked with the guy for eleven years . . . and he just kind of like walked, took off."

The whole point of a band is that you're in it together: blood in; blood out. You've made a commitment that the only way you're leaving is in a pine box. That's why we told Ted to fuck off right at the beginning when he wanted us to replace our singer. That's why I convinced Ed to stick it out when he wanted to leave in '82. For Dave to leave when the public had voted in favor of us as a group . . . it just felt like treason. Like really dumb treason. Like premature evacuation!

"Everybody in the band felt let down," Dave wrote. "Everybody in the band felt abandoned. I felt the same thing that they were feeling. Two opposites become the exact same thing. 'Well, Dave was working on something else.' 'No, that's what Ed was doing.'" It's no problem seeing what's messed up about the other guy. It's a lot harder to see what you're doing wrong yourself. Marriage is easy compared to keeping four grown men together through year after year of nonstop traveling, performing, promoting, and recording. Especially when one of them is your younger brother and another is an egomaniac!

On the one hand we were glad Dave was gone because he was so far up his own ass. But artistically, you just feel something is amiss.

Something is not right.

We had a lot of other singers over the years. We had more success later on, when we finally got the manager we deserved in Ed Leffler. (Yet another guy I miss. He couldn't have been better to us . . . or better at his job . . . or a better guy, period. See you on the other side, Leffler.)

But creativity is an argument among friends. And we never fought better with anyone than we did with Dave.

It was like we put all of our ideas together in a dogfight and whichever ones got out alive made it onstage. "If that conflict gnawed away at all of us constantly, out of it came earthshaking, culture-changing music," Dave wrote. He's right, it's undeniable.

Dave was the first guy I called after Ed passed, the first guy I wanted to talk to. Just out of mutual respect for what we had done together with my brother, who neither of us will ever get to work with again in this lifetime.

THE TWO EVENTS ARE NOT of the same magnitude, but the *feelings* that I experienced when Dave bailed—of unfairness, of anger, loss, and bafflement with the workings of the universe—were like a preview of the oceanic grief that came over me when my brother passed. And there was that familiar sense of a terrible outcome somehow happening both incrementally and abruptly. Don't get me wrong: there's *no comparison*. (The first thing is a papercut. The second is getting your head cut off.) After Dave quit Van Halen, we moved on; it wasn't the end of the world, or even the band. In terms of my brother, it's taken me about a year to write this book; it's been almost four years now since he died. I still wake up most mornings and think, *Ed! Where the fuck are you?* I'll never get over it. I'll never say goodbye.

I find myself thinking about the beginning a lot these days. In some ways, the distant past feels more vivid than what happened last week! I have dreams about the boat ride here from Holland . . . playing piano in the banquet hall with the boat smell, and hoping to see that dark-haired little girl. Pasadena, California—the promised land! Those syllables and sounds, so thoroughly devoid of Dutch. And the colors! My uncle's baby-blue Ford; oranges for a penny. The Broken Combs. My mom with her purse full of steak. Throwing a bottle at Red Ball Jet. The stabbing at Walter Mitty's. Electric Lady with Gene. Sprinting off the Ventura Freeway in platform shoes to get to our big meeting at Warner Bros. That night in Scotland when we found out we'd gone gold! The gold records my cousin stole from Las Lunas Street. Searching for Ozzy in the stairwells; watching him blast those duck decoys out of his pond. Castaic Lake with Gregg and Ed and my old man, who were all alive that day, and aren't anymore. Ed's wedding— the drunkest I've ever seen him. The first time he played me the riff from "Jump." That night in Nuremberg, Germany, the last show of our last tour as the original Van Halen.

"We sold the idea of imagination," Dave wrote, "*extreme* imagination, *forced* to the breaking point." And we broke. It was the most disappointing thing I'd experienced in my life, the thing that seemed the most wasteful and unjust.

Until I lost my brother.

CODA

They could finish each other's sentences . . . have a
whole conversation without talking, at times. Or
they were throwing a Dutch word here or there, an
expression. They were like twins, Ed and Al. With
twins there is this kind of unspoken understanding.
This incredible trust. They had each other's backs.

—STINE VAN HALEN, 2022

It's your birthday today, Ed: January 26, 2024. You would be sixty-nine.

The outpouring of grief is ongoing. Someone posted this morning, "I'm so sorry Alex. I NEVER EVER cried for someone I never knew, but it felt like I knew you both, as many of us grew up on your music and went to every concert when Van Halen came to town. . . . Music hasn't been the same without Ed." Amen!

Someone else wrote, "Alex, you and your brother saved my life when I was in a really dark period. Thank you for inspiring me and helping me through so many dark days." Forget the Grammys, forget the Billboard *chart, forget the Rock & Roll Hall of Fame. What a privilege to connect with a stranger through our music on that level. Isn't that the point of art? It makes life more bearable. Art is hope.*

This one is my favorite, though: "Sending you the best energies, Al—Eddie was a hero of mine and my wife also died of cancer a year after him. Living one day after the other here . . . love stays." That it does.

Anger, too. Cancer killed you, but a lifetime of drinking and drugs didn't help, Ed. When you first got cancer, on your tongue, you blamed it on years of holding a metal guitar pick in your mouth while you played—instead of on the three cigarettes at a time you smoked all day long for thirty years! What the hell kind of insanity is that? Just thinking about it works me up.

We had a dream that millions of people dream—but for us it came true! Do you know how lucky we are?! Do you know how fortunate you were to be born with a talent?

And maybe you never believed you were worthy of your gift, and that's why you were so self-destructive. Every artist can relate to that. At one point or another you want to smash your instrument, cut off your ear, bang your head against the wall like the guy on the cover of Fair Warning! *You want to destroy the thing that's the most precious to you, so you can stop holding on to it for dear life, stop worrying about it disappearing. But you were brave until the end, Ed.*

If anyone thinks you were just a partier, an addict, an alcoholic, they don't understand how difficult it is to get to the place where your inhibitions are down and you can just create. *Jimi Hendrix, Janis Joplin, Kurt Cobain, Edward Van Halen. They didn't all just happen to have bad judgment or weak willpower. They drank or snorted or shot up whatever potion they'd chosen because they were trying to get out of reality, the realm of logic, the everyday. The road is littered with musicians who died pursuing what they thought they heard. In our line of work, addiction is an occupational hazard.*

The industry joke was: you'll never see both Van Halen brothers sober at the same time. For years it was the truth! Alcohol used to blunt any overthinking and I could just be totally in the moment, in the flow, let my body take over. But it got to a point where I knew I'd burn myself out if I didn't stop.

You never stopped. The real problem isn't that you drank alcohol, it's that you drank the Kool-Aid: people telling you you're a genius, that you're the greatest guitar player who ever lived. All true. But you ate it up, and then you were overwhelmed by the burden of it.

Our dad told us from the beginning: Don't believe your own bullshit. Just play. And if you're playing a wedding, wear a tux! Give it everything you've got. Fulfill your obligations: you are the head of the family! Do your JOB.

But love stays.

That's the truth. We still communicate. Paul McCartney once said of John Lennon, "I now will often think, if I'm writing a song, Okay, John—I'll toss it over to you. What line comes next? So I've got a virtual John." I know what he means. You're still with me, Ed.

Because we live in a Western society, people want to dismiss that as a projection. But ask any physicist: energy can be neither created nor destroyed. When a cloud dissipates, what happens to the water? It isn't gone. It's just changed form. The same thing goes for you, Ed, or any other human being on this planet.

So I'll never say goodbye.

As I get older, I'm getting more superstitious, like Mom—the islander in me is coming out! (I turned seventy, by the way: I'm in my frigging SEVENTIES. If you were here my only consolation would be giving you shit because you'd be joining me in this decade SOON.) I think about how our mother died on my younger son Malcolm's birthday, August 4, and then you died on my older son Aric's, October 6. I don't know what that means, exactly, but I don't think you can write that off as coincidence. Same thing with our first bassist, Mark Stone, dying ten days before you did. Or the time I called Gregg Emerson—after years and years of being out of touch—to tell him, "Hey! I just had a son!" And he replied, "You're kidding, so did I." There's something about souls traveling in and out of this life together.

I know I'll see you again. And we'll jam for hours—for days. That was always our most intense form of intimacy, and you never, ever pulled rank. You never said—or even thought—"You're just the drummer, Al, and I'm the world's greatest guitarist, so we're doing it my way." We were equals, and you never forgot that. We supported each other unconditionally, no matter how much we fought. We were a team.

We were brothers. We're still brothers. Even death can't change that.

Paul McCartney said something else I like: "The Beatles were brothers arguing. That's what families do."

I'll see you again, Ed.

And when I do, I'm going to kick your ass.

Love,

Al

AUTHOR'S NOTE

I relied on my memories to write this book, and I'm glad that some of the other people who were there when all of this was going on wrote down their own. *Runnin' with the Devil* by the late Noel Monk and *A Platinum Producer's Life in Music* by Ted Templeman were both interesting reads, and then, of course, there was *Crazy from the Heat* by David Lee Roth, which reminded me of incidents and conversations I hadn't thought about in years. I disagree with my former collaborators on all sorts of things, but I was still interested to hear their various sides of the story. I have mixed feelings about the books by all the Van Halen–ologists because they weren't actually *there*, but I read them all just to remind myself of everything Ed and I said over the years—sometimes when we were angry, sometimes when we'd had a few, and sometimes when we managed to put into words what we were always better at saying through our music.

ACKNOWLEDGMENTS

THANK YOU, Stine, Aric, Malcolm, Wolf, Ed, Jan and Eugenia Van Halen, Ariel Levy, Luke Janklow, Irving Azoff, Sara Nelson, Edie Astley, Ben Pfeiffer, Charlie Arneson, Rupert Handgretinger, Thomas Vogl, Bill Wilson, Joe Walsh, Larry Solters, Mo Ostin, Ted Templeman, Donn Landee, Ed Leffler, Lenny Waronker, Glenn Ballard, Ross Hogarth, John Shanks, Hans Zimmer, Bob Clearmountain, Johnny Douglas, Brad "1.5" Stark, John Beug, Carolyn Mayer, Billy Carson, Mark Fenske, Michael Karlin, Susan Genco, Harry Sandler, Kristen Price, Rafi Anteby, John McEnroe, Roy Schmidt Weymans, Heinz Pasche, Matt Sencio, Neil Zlozower, Stan Getz, Freddy Gruber, Jim Keltner, Levon Helm, Simon Phillips, Billy Cobham, Hal Blaine, Buddy Rich, Ringo Starr, Dave Clark, Louis Bellson, Art Blakey, Max Roach, Elvin Jones, Joe Morello, Ginger Baker, Keith Moon, John Bonham, Ed Shaughnessy, Max Thoms, Terry Bozzio, Jeff, Steve and Mike Porcaro, Kenny Aronoff, Mike Portnoy, David Garibaldi, Jim Keltner, Carmine Appice, Bill Bruford, Vinnie Colaiuto, Steve Lukather, Brian May, Jimmy Page, Les Paul, David Paich, Gene Simmons, Paul Stanley, Ozzy Osbourne, Tony Iommi, David Lee Roth, Nathan Roth, Lars Ulrich, Rodney Bingenheimer, Gregg Emerson, Neal Schon, Chris Cornell, Billy Sheehan, Rick Granati, George Gaspar, Paul "Jamo" Jaimeson, Ross Velasco, Kennis Lutz, Denis Imler, Eddie Anderson, Charlie Sheen, Ken Deane, Ross Hogarth, Todd Trent, Bill Ludwig III, Ken Micallef, David Frangioni, Dave Weiderman, Peggy McCreary,

Dweezil Zappa, Brian Kehew, Mark and Darlene Stone, Tommy Robbie, Rick Broderick, Terry Kilgore, Dana Anderson, Dan Stewart, Mike Palomo, Brian and Kevin Hill, Don Ferris, John Heil, Richie Mahaffey, Robin Williams, Kevin Ford, Frank Trejo, Stan Swantek, Larry Abajian, Jennifer Blakeman, Liz Wiley, Mike Ascolese, James Borrelli, and GOD.